Berlitz
Basic French

Course Book

Berlitz Publishing
New York   London   Singapore

No part of this book may be reproduced, stored in a retrieval system or transmitted in any form or means electronic, mechanical, photocopying, recording or otherwise, without prior written permission from APA Publications.

Contacting the Editors
Every effort has been made to provide accurate information in this publication, but changes are inevitable. The publisher cannot be responsible for any resulting loss, inconvenience or injury. We would appreciate it if readers would call our attention to any errors or outdated information. We also welcome your suggestions.
Please contact us at: comments@berlitzpublishing.com

All Rights Reserved
© 2003 Berlitz Publishing/APA Publications (UK) Ltd.
Berlitz Trademark Reg. U.S. Patent Office and other countries. Marca Registrada. Used under license from Berlitz Investment Corporation.

Cover and pack redesign © April 2012
Printed in China

Senior Commissioning Editor: Kate Drynan
Audio Producer: Paul Ruben Studio
Text: Rosi McNab
Cover Design: Beverley Speight
Interior Design: Max Crandall
Production Manager: Vicky Glover
Opener Illustrations: Andy Levine
Illustrations: Max Crandall, Mona Daly, Elise Dodeles, Andy Levine, Chris Reed, Isabelle Verret
Maps: MAGELLAN Geographix, Parrot Graphics

Contents

Unit 1   **Bonjour Monsieur, Bonjour Madame!** *Meeting, greeting, and introducing yourself; spelling; days and dates; numbers 0–20* 1

     Lesson 1 (Track 1) **Bonjour!** 2

     Lesson 2 (Track 2) **Je suis** 6

     Lesson 3 (Track 3) **A l'hôtel** 12

     Extra (Track 4) A1

     Checkpoints 16

Unit 2   **Vous désirez?** *Eating out and shopping; numbers 21–99 and 100–1000* 19

     Lesson 1 (Track 5) **Au café** 20

     Lesson 2 (Track 6) **A la brasserie** 24

     Lesson 3 (Track 7) **Chez le marchand de journaux** 29

     Extra (Track 8) A4

     Checkpoints 34

Unit 3   **Au travail et en famille** *Holding a conversation; small talk; professions and workplaces; family life* 37

     Lesson 1 (Track 1) **Quel est votre métier?** 38

     Lesson 2 (Track 2) **Une photo de ma famille** 43

     Lesson 3 (Track 3) **Qu'est-ce qu'on va faire?** 48

     Extra (Track 4) A7

     Checkpoints 52

Test 1   ***Review of Units 1–3*** B1

Unit 4

En ville *Finding your way around town; making plans; opening and closing times* **55**

Lesson 1 (Track 5) **Il y a une banque près d'ici?** **56**

Lesson 2 (Track 6) **Pour aller à … ?** **60**

Lesson 3 (Track 7) **Vous fermez à quelle heure?** **64**

Extra (Track 8) **A9**

Checkpoints **68**

Unit 5

Au centre commercial *Shopping for a variety of goods; choosing clothing; size and color; comparing items* **71**

Lesson 1 (Track 1) **A la pharmacie** **72**

Lesson 2 (Track 2) **Vous désirez?** **75**

Lesson 3 (Track 3) **A la caisse** **79**

Extra (Track 4) **A10**

Checkpoints **84**

Unit 6

Les moyens de transport *Methods of travel; using public transportation; how to rent a car* **87**

Lesson 1 (Track 5) **Comment allez-vous au travail?** **88**

Lesson 2 (Track 6) **On prend le bus ou le métro?** **92**

Lesson 3 (Track 7) **Prendre un taxi ou louer une voiture?** **97**

Extra (Track 8) **A12**

Checkpoints **102**

Test 2

Review of Units 4–6 .... **B5**

Answer Key **C1**

Bonjour Monsieur! Bonjour Madame!

1

Word Bank

une baguette	*a long French loaf*	deux	*two*
le boulanger	*the baker*	oui	*yes*
un croissant	*a croissant*	mais	*but*
et	*and*	non	*no*
le nom	*name*	six	*six*
votre	*your*	un/une	*a/one*

Bonjour!

Greeting people and saying how you are

1. *Listen to these four short conversations and write down what time of day it is and whether or not the speakers know each other.*

a. daytime

b. early evening

c. late evening

Bonjour	*good day*
Bonsoir	*good evening*
Bonne nuit	*good night, used late evening, when going to bed*
Au revoir	*good-bye*
Salut!	*Hi! used both as a greeting and farewell*

2. *Listen to M. Albert greeting these people. Who is he talking to? Write the number of each conversation on the line below the corresponding illustration. Notice that in France you always add* **Monsieur, Madame,** *etc., when greeting someone or saying goodbye.*

a. _____ b. _____ c. _____ d. _____ e. _____

Monsieur (M.)	*Mr./Sir*
Madame (Mme)	*Mrs./Madam*
Mademoiselle (Mlle)	*Miss/young lady*
Messieursdames	*Ladies and gentlemen*
Messieurs (MM.)	*Gentlemen*
Mesdames	*Ladies*

3. M. Albert is the baker. Listen to these people coming into his shop and write the number of the conversation beside each picture. What do they buy?

a.

b.

c.

d.

Chez le boulanger	At the baker's
Merci.	Thank you.
S'il vous plaît.	Please.
Voilà.	Here you are.

4. Listen to the conversations again and put a (✓) beside each picture if the speaker is well, (−) if the speaker is okay, and (✗) if the speaker is not so well.

Comment ça va?	How are you? (lit: How goes it?)
Ça va.	Okay (lit: It goes).
Ça va bien merci, et vous?	Well, thank you, and you?
Pas mal.	Not bad/okay.
Comme ci, comme ça.	So so.

5. *Et vous? Comment ça va?* What would you say?

6. *Now it's your turn to ask these people how they are. Complete the conversations by filling in the missing words where you see _____. Put your name where you see _____.*

_____ Duval!

Bonjour _____! Comment ça va?

_____. Et vous?

_____.

Au revoir _____.

Au revoir _____ Duval.

_____ Meugeot.

Bonsoir _____. Ça va?

_____. Et vous? Ça va?

Oui, merci. Au revoir _____.

Au revoir _____ Meugeot.

_____ Renoir.

Bonsoir _____.

Ça va?

_____. Je vais me coucher. Bonne nuit!

_____ _____ Renoir.

Je vais me coucher.   I am going to bed.

Pronunciation

As French is not always pronounced as it is written, you need to spend a little extra time, especially at the beginning, practicing pronunciation and intonation. For this reason, we have added some short pronunciation tips and exercises in each unit.

Listen carefully and repeat the following words, trying to imitate the pronunciation:

monsieur   **messieursdames**

messieurs   **mademoiselle**

madame   **mesdemoiselles**

mesdames

In French all syllables are stressed equally. Listen carefully and repeat these words, remembering to stress both parts of the word:

Mon/sieur   **Bon/jour**   **Ba/guette**

Ma/dame   **Crois/sant**

Learning tips

Quite a few letters are not pronounced all the time in French. Listen to the dialogs carefully. You may find it helpful to write down how a word sounds to you to help you remember it. For example, you might think **monsieur** sounds like "mus-yer."

Don't worry if you can't remember everything yet. You'll have many more opportunities to practice!

Close-up

In French all nouns are either masculine or feminine.

The word for "a/one" before masculine nouns is **un**:

un croissant   a/one croissant

Before feminine nouns it is **une**:

une baguette   a/one baguette

To make the plural most French nouns add an **s**:

deux baguette**s**

deux croissant**s**

Note that the **s** is not pronounced.

Je suis ...

I am ...

Word Bank

à	at/in	les Etats-Unis	the United States
Comment?	How?	aux Etats-Unis	in the United States
en	in	la France	France
la conférence	conference	en France	in France
Où?	Where?	l'Italie *f.*	Italy
Voici ...	Here is ...	en Italie	in Italy
*être	to be	le Japon	Japan
l'Allemagne *f.*	Germany	au Japon	in Japan
en Allemagne	in Germany	la Suisse	Switzerland
l'Angleterre *f.*	England	en Suisse	in Switzerland
en Angleterre	in England	américain/américaine	American
les Antilles	the Antilles (West Indies)	anglais/anglaise	English
aux Antilles	in the West Indies	belge	Belgian
la Belgique	Belgium	brésilien/brésilienne	Brazilian
en Belgique	in Belgium	canadien/canadienne	Canadian
le Brésil	Brazil	espagnol/espagnole	Spanish
au Brésil	in Brazil	français/française	French
le Canada	Canada	italien/italienne	Italian
au Canada	in Canada	japonais/japonaise	Japanese
l'Espagne *f.*	Spain	portugais/portugaise	Portuguese
en Espagne	in Spain	suisse	Swiss

*irregular verbs are indicated with an asterisk

1. *These people are attending an international conference in Paris. Listen to M. Martin asking them who they are and where they are from, then match up the names with the countries.*

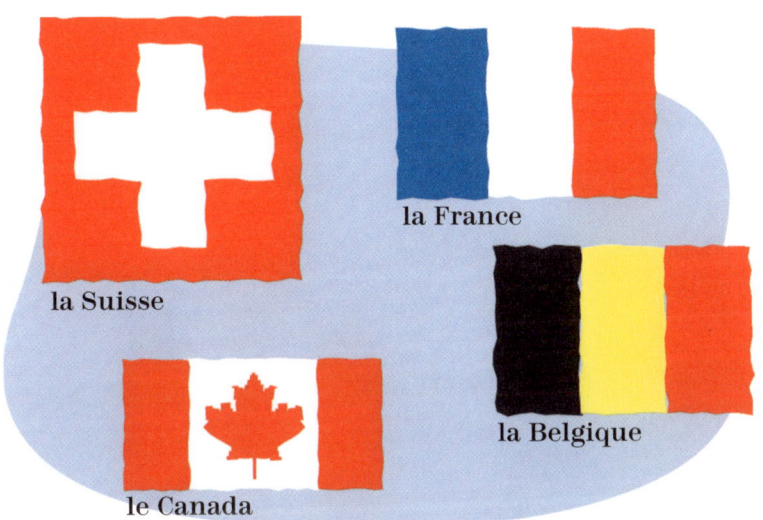

- *a.* Gilles Bernard
- *b.* Sylvie Verlaine
- *c.* Lucienne Briand
- *d.* Patrice Millerioux

J'habite …	*I live …*
Je m'appelle …	*My name is …*
Je suis …	*I am …*

2. *Prepare what you would say to introduce these four people to a French colleague. Write it down in your notebook.*

Je vous présente M. Gilles Bernard. Il est _____ et il habite à _____ en _____. Voici Mme Briand. Elle est _____ et elle habite _____.

Sometimes the adjective changes for the feminine form. Check that you are using the right form of the adjective. For example, you would say: **M. Millerioux est <u>canadien</u>**, *but if you were talking about his wife you would say:* **Mme Millerioux est <u>canadienne</u>**.

RECORDING

3. *Sylvie Verlaine hasn't been paying attention and is asking you about the delegates. If she is right say* **Oui, il est _____** *(if she is talking about a man) or* **Oui, elle est _____** *(if she is talking about a woman). If she is wrong say* **Non, il/elle n'est pas _____, il/elle est _____**.

Example: M. Bernard est américain?
Non, il n'est pas américain, il est suisse.

Vrai ou faux?   *True or false?*

4. *Listen to these five contestants on a television quiz show. Where is each one from? What languages does each one speak? Complete the sentences.*

a. Bonjour. Je m'appelle Gérard et je suis _____.
J'habite à Rouen et je parle français et _____ .

b. Moi? Je _____ Anja et je _____ allemande.
J'_____ à Berlin _____ Allemagne. Je parle allemand et un peu _____.

c. J' _____ à New York _____ Etats-Unis. Je m'appelle Nigel _____ je suis _____. Je ne _____ pas français.

d. Je m'appelle Kenji et j'habite à Tokyo _____ Japon. Je _____ japonais et je parle japonais et _____.

e. Moi? Je m'appelle _____. Non, je ne suis pas espagnole. Je suis brésilienne. J'habite à _____ au _____. Je parle portugais, anglais et _____ de français.

un peu (de)   *a little (of)*

5. **A vous!** *Now it's your turn. The presenter is asking you some questions. What is he asking? How would you answer?*

Unit 1   9

6. *How would you ask this young woman and this young man about themselves?*

7. *Now see if you can introduce yourself, give your name, say where you live, and tell what nationality you are. Complete the sentences.*

Je m'appelle _____.

J'habite à en/au/aux _____.

Je suis _____.

Pronunciation

Some pairs of words are pronounced as one, for example: **Etats-Unis, au revoir.** *Listen carefully and repeat each phrase.*

Listen to these phrases and practice saying them. Remember to stress all the syllables and to pronounce the words as one, where indicated.

Marc habite au Canada.

Jon habite aux Etats-Unis.

Lucy habite en Angleterre.

Lee habite au Japon.

Close-up

The word for "the" with masculine nouns is **le**:
le nom   the name   le Canada   Canada

and with feminine nouns it is **la**:
la France   France   la Belgique   Belgium

If the noun begins with a vowel or "h" (m. and f.) you use **l'**:
l'hôtel *m.*   the hotel   l'Amérique *f.*   America

The plural for both m. and f. is **les**:
les chambres *f.* the rooms   les Etats-Unis *m.* the United States

The word for "in"
a. With feminine countries use **en**:
b. With the names of towns and cities use **à**:
c. With masculine and plural countries use **à**:

    à + le = au   J'habite au Canada.
    à + les = aux   J'habite aux Etats-Unis.

Saying what nationality you are

If you are a man: Je suis américain/français.   I am American/French.
If you are a woman: Je suis américaine/française.   I am American/French.

The names of the languages are the same as the masculine form:
    Je parle français.   Je parle anglais.

Pronouns

Singular		Plural	
je	I	nous	we
tu	you	vous	you
il	he	ils	they
elle	she	elles	they

Elles *is used only when talking about two or more females. If the company is mixed you have to use* **ils**.

*être	to be		
je suis	I am	nous sommes	we are
tu es	you are	vous êtes	you are
il est	he is	ils sont	they are
elle est	she is	elles sont	they are

The negative

To make a negative in French you add **ne** (or **n'** before a vowel) in front of the verb and **pas** after the verb:

Vous êtes suisse?   Non, je ne suis pas suisse.
Il est japonais?   Non, il n'est pas japonais.

À l'hôtel

Checking into a hotel

Numbers 1-20

1	un	11	onze
2	deux	12	douze
3	trois	13	treize
4	quatre	14	quatorze
5	cinq	15	quinze
6	six	16	seize
7	sept	17	dix-sept
8	huit	18	dix-huit
9	neuf	19	dix-neuf
10	dix	20	vingt

Word Bank

la chambre	*room/bedroom*	la salle de bains	*bathroom*
la douche	*shower*	la société	*company/business*
l'hôtel *m.*	*hotel*	s'il vous plaît	*please*
le nombre	*number*	ou	*or*
la réception	*reception*	venir	*to come*
la réservation	*reservation*		

1. *Listen to this group of tourists at the reception desk of your hotel. The guide is reading out their names to the clerk. Number the names in the order in which you hear them.*

Fernandez	Macintosh	Schwartz
Graham	Rossellini	

à la réception	at the reception desk
Comment ça s'écrit?	How do you spell it?
C'est exact.	That's right.
Je vous en prie.	You're welcome.

2. *The clerk has not heard some of the names properly and asks you to spell them again for her. Spell them aloud.*

3. *Listen to the alphabet and pick out the letters you need to spell your own name. Write down the sound of the letters you find difficult, for example "e" sounds like "uh."*

Votre nom, s'il vous plaît?	What is your name, please?

4. *Now you check in. Listen to the clerk's questions and answer them. Use the following phrases if you don't understand or if she is talking too fast.*

Je ne comprends pas.	I don't understand.
Parlez plus lentement, s'il vous plaît.	Please speak more slowly.
Vous avez une réservation?	Do you have a reservation?
Vous venez d'où?	Where are you from? (lit: you come from where?)
Vous voulez une chambre avec douche ou salle de bain?	Do you want a room with shower or bathroom (meaning with a bathtub)?

Unit 1   13

5.

The clerk is telling guests their room numbers. Listen and write them down.

a. Fernandez est à la chambre numéro _____.

b. Macintosh est à la chambre numéro _____.

c. Schwartz est à la chambre numéro _____.

d. Rossellini est à la chambre numéro _____.

e. Graham est à la chambre numéro _____.

| C'est la chambre numéro … | It's room number … |

6.

The tour guide needs to distribute the program for the visit. Tell him which rooms everybody is in. Read the names and numbers aloud.

| Il/Elle est à quelle chambre? | Which room is he/she in? |
| Il/Elle est à la chambre numéro … | He/she is in room number … |

7.

Imagine you are calling Société Beauvin and asking to speak to M. Duval. Listen to Martin Smith doing it first.

Au téléphone	On the telephone
Allô?	Hello?
Je peux parler avec … ?	Can I speak to … ?
C'est de la part de qui?	Who is speaking? (lit: it's on the behalf of whom?)
Vous pouvez épeler?	Can you spell (it)?
Ne quittez pas!	Hold on!

Pronunciation

Accents are used with some letters in French to modify their sound. The accents are called:

accent aigu	**é**
accent grave	**à è ù**
cédille	**ç**
accent circonflexe	**â ê î ô û**

é *is pronounced "ay," as in* **écrit**, **activité**.

è *is pronounced "eh," as in* **frère**, *brother,* **Frère Jacques**, *Brother James.*

ç *before a, o, and u is pronounced like "s" in "so":* **Ça va**, **français**, **garçon**.

The accent circonflexe does not change the sound.

The letters **s** *and* **t** *at the end of a word are not usually pronounced:* **vou(s)**, **nui(t)**, **françai(s)**.

When **s** *is followed by* **e** *it is pronounced:*
Il est français. *(s is not sounded)* **Elle est française.** *(s is sounded)*

Listen carefully and repeat these phrases:

Il est français. Elle est française.

Il est anglais. Elle est anglaise.

Il est japonais. Elle est japonaise.

Close-up

Rappel! *The word for "the" with masculine nouns is* **le** *and with feminine nouns it is* **la**: **le nom**, **la chambre**.

If the word begins with a vowel or "h" (m. and f.) use **l'**: **l'hôtel**, **l'Amérique**.

The plural for both m. and f. nouns is **les**: **les noms**, **les chambres**.

	m.	f.	pl.
a/one	**un**	**une**	**des** (some)
the	**le (l')**	**la (l')**	**les**

Checkpoints

Use the check list to test what you've learned in this unit and review anything you're not sure of.

Can you ... ? Yes No

- *say good morning (to a man)* .... ❏ ..... ❏
  Bonjour monsieur.

- *good evening (to a woman)* .... ❏ ..... ❏
  Bonsoir madame.

- *good night (to a young woman)* .... ❏ ..... ❏
  Bonne nuit mademoiselle.

- *goodbye (to a group)* .... ❏ ..... ❏
  Au revoir messieursdames.

- *ask someone how (s)he is* .... ❏ ..... ❏
  Ça va?

- *and say you are well, thank you* .... ❏ ..... ❏
  Ça va bien, merci.

- *say you are okay* .... ❏ ..... ❏
  Ça va.

- *say you are not bad* .... ❏ ..... ❏
  Pas mal.

- *say you are not so well* .... ❏ ..... ❏
  Ça ne va pas.

- *say what your name is* .... ❏ ..... ❏
  Je m'appelle ...

- *what nationality you are* .... ❏ ..... ❏
  Je suis ...

- *where you live* .... ❏ ..... ❏
  J'habite ...

- *what languages you speak* .... ❏ ..... ❏
  Je parle ...

- *ask people what their names are* .... ❏ ..... ❏
  Comment vous appelez-vous?

- *if they live in (Paris)* .... ❏ ..... ❏
  Vous habitez à Paris?

- *if they speak (French)* .... ❏ ..... ❏
  Parlez-vous français?

Can you ... ?   Yes   No

- *ask some people if they are (American)* .... ❑ ...... ❑
  Vous êtes américain(e)?

- *say you don't understand* .... ❑ ...... ❑
  Je ne comprends pas.

- *ask someone to speak more slowly* .... ❑ ...... ❑
  Parlez plus lentement, s'il vous plaît.

- *ask someone how to write/spell something* .... ❑ ...... ❑
  Comment ça s'écrit?
  Vous pouvez épeler?

- *say the numbers 0–20* .... ❑ ...... ❑

- *say please* .... ❑ ...... ❑
  S'il vous plaît.

Learning tips

Try to spend a few minutes each day listening to the dialogs so that you become more familiar with the sound of French. You may find it difficult at first to distinguish individual words, but don't be discouraged. Keep listening and you will soon be able to recognize what is being said, which is the first step in learning a new language.

Rappel! *Remember: always add* **Monsieur**, **Madame**, *etc., when greeting someone or saying goodbye.*

Do you want to learn more?

Do you have access to French language newspapers or magazines? If so, turn to the foreign news section and see how many country names you can recognize. If you don't have access, the French consulate or the national tourist offices may be able to help you.

For more practice, see Extra! on page A1.

Unit 2 is about learning how to:
- order drinks in a café
- buy refreshments in a brasserie
- make small purchases at a newsstand

Vous désirez? 2

Word Bank

l'addition *f.*	*bill*	l'express *m.*	*espresso*
la bière	*beer*	le jus d'orange	*orange juice*
le café	*coffee*	du lait	*some milk*
le chocolat chaud	*hot chocolate*	l'orange pressée	*freshly squeezed orange*
le Coca®	*Coke®*		
le crème	*coffee light*	le thé	*tea*
le croissant	*croissant*	le thé au lait	*tea with milk*
le déca	*decaffeinated coffee*	grand	*big*
de l'eau (minérale)	*some (mineral) water*	petit	*small*
gazeuse	*sparkling/carbonated*		
non gazeuse	*still (noncarbonated)*		

Au café

At the café

M. and Mme Albert are at a café in Rouen with their daughters Nathalie and Delphine. Listen to them ordering drinks. What did they each decide to have?

Vous désirez?
What would you like?

Je voudrais …
I would like …

pour moi/pour toi
for me/for you

Avez-vous … ?
Have you … ?

bien sûr
of course

C'est tout?
Is that everything?/Anything else?

tout de suite
right away

Un café *is a small black coffee,* **un express** *is an espresso, and* **un crème** *is a coffee light (with a lot of milk or cream). You will often be offered a choice of large or small crème:* **"Grand ou petit?"**

Garçon, *which means "boy," was once used to signal the waiter. Today, to attract the waiter's attention, you should say* **Monsieur** *or, for a waitress,* **Madame** *or* **Mademoiselle**.

Now you are going to hear some of the other people in the café. What do they order?

alors — then

Je n'ai plus de croissants. — *I don't have any croissants left.*

RECORDING 3.

You are in a café in France with some friends, who want you to order for them. Write down a list of what they want and then practice what you would say to the waiter.

Example: I would like a fresh orange juice.
Je voudrais une orange pressée.

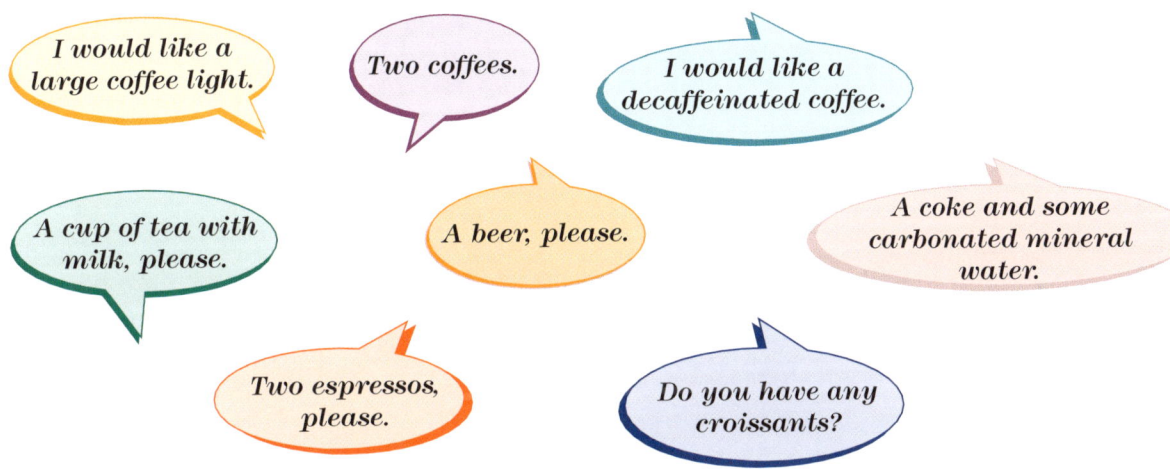

- I would like a large coffee light.
- Two coffees.
- I would like a decaffeinated coffee.
- A cup of tea with milk, please.
- A beer, please.
- A coke and some carbonated mineral water.
- Two espressos, please.
- Do you have any croissants?

Now listen to see if you got it right. Repeat the phrases to practice pronunciation and intonation.

RECORDING 4.

Listen and learn the numbers 20 through 60. Repeat each number after you hear it.

Numbers 20–60

20 vingt	25 vingt-cinq	30 trente
21 vingt et un	26 vingt-six	40 quarante
22 vingt-deux	27 vingt-sept	50 cinquante
23 vingt-trois	28 vingt-huit	60 soixante
24 vingt-quatre	29 vingt-neuf	

Unit 2   21

These are the winning numbers in the lottery this week. How would you say them in French?

5. *Now it's time for M. Albert to pay. Listen to find out how he asks for the bill. How much does he have to pay?*

Ça fait combien?	How much is it?
Ça fait …	That's …
Tenez (c'est pour vous).	There you are (that's for you). (when giving someone a tip)
Bonne journée.	Have a nice day.

6. *Fill in the gaps in this conversation in the restaurant. Order the items given in English using the phrases you have learned and ask for the bill.*

Garçon: Vous désirez?

You: *(Ask if they have any mineral water.)*

Garçon: Gazeuse ou non gazeuse?

You: *(Sparkling please.)*

Garçon: C'est tout?

You: *(You would like a coffee light.)*

Garçon: Grand ou petit?

You: *(A large one.)*

Pronunciation

Listen carefully to distinguish between the pronunciation of **un** and **une**. Write down what they sound like if you find that helpful.

Now practice saying these words:

un thé	**une bière**
un café	**une orange**

Remember how some groups of words are pronounced as one. Listen and repeat these phrases:

C'est tout?

Tout de suite.

S'il vous plaît.

Close-up

Rappel! To make the plural, you usually add **s** to the end of the word, as in English:

un crème	deux crème<u>s</u>
un café	deux café<u>s</u>

But the **s** ending is not pronounced.

All nouns in French are either masculine or feminine.

The definite article "the" and indefinite article "a" have different forms in French depending on whether the noun is masculine or feminine:

With masculine words:	With feminine words:
<u>un</u> café . . . . . . a coffee	<u>une</u> bière . . . . a beer
<u>le</u> café . . . . . the coffee	<u>la</u> bière . . . . the beer

Use **l'** before words that begin with a vowel or "h":

<u>un</u> hôtel . . . . . . a hotel   l'hôtel . . . . the hotel

A la brasserie

At the brasserie

Word Bank

la boisson	*drink*
la bouteille (de vin rouge/blanc)	*bottle (of red/white wine)*
la crème Chantilly	*vanilla-flavored sweetened whipped cream*
le dessert	*dessert*
le fromage	*cheese*
la glace	*ice cream*
à la fraise	*strawberry flavored*
à la vanille	*vanilla flavored*
à la banane	*banana flavored*
au chocolat	*chocolate flavored*
aux pistaches	*pistachio flavored*
le hamburger	*hamburger*
le milk-shake	*milkshake*
l'omelette f.	*omelet*
aux fines herbes	*with mixed herbs*
nature	*plain*
au jambon	*with ham*
le pichet (de vin)	*jug (of wine)*
la portion de frites	*portion of fries*
une bière pression	*draft beer*
la salade	*salad*
niçoise	*with tuna and olives*
de fruits de mer	*seafood salad*
aux trois fromages	*with three cheeses*
le sandwich	*sandwich*
le saucisson	*sausage/salami*
un steak frites	*steak and fries*
la tarte aux pommes	*apple pie*
le thé au citron	*tea with lemon*
le verre (de vin)	*glass (of wine)*
le vin (rouge/blanc)	*(red/white) wine*
aussi	*also*
avec	*with*
rien	*nothing*

RECORDING 1.

Listen to these two customers in the brasserie. What sort of sandwiches are available? What do they order to eat and drink?

Qu'est-ce que vous avez comme (sandwichs)?
What sort of (sandwiches) do you have?

un sandwich au jambon/au fromage/au saucisson
a ham/cheese/sausage sandwich

Et comme boisson?
And to drink?

> **Did You Know?**
>
> **Brasseries** were originally places where you could buy beer, but now they have become popular eating places where you can get a quick meal without paying restaurant prices.

2. **A vous!** *What would you say to find out what sort of sandwiches are available? How would you ask what sort of salads are on the menu? And what sort of ice cream?*

RECORDING 3.

Now you choose something for yourself and a friend. Write down what you would order, then practice aloud what you would say.

> Waiter: Messieursdames, vous désirez?
>
> You: Je voudrais _____ pour moi et _____ pour mon ami(e).
>
> Waiter: Et comme boisson?
>
> You: Je voudrais _____ pour moi et _____ pour mon ami(e).

mon ami(e)   *my friend*

RECORDING 4.

Listen to the other people in the brasserie giving their orders and write down what they would like.

Et avec ça?   *Anything else? (lit: and with that?)*

En bouteille ou pression?   *Bottle or draft?*

Unit 2

RECORDING 5.

Now listen to find out what desserts they choose. Which would you choose for yourself and a friend? How would you order?

Vous voulez … ?   Do you want … ?

Merci.*   Thank you.

Moi aussi.   Me too.

* *Warning!* **Merci** *means "No thank you" when you have been offered something. If you want what you have been offered say:* **S'il vous plaît.**

RECORDING 6.

Listen and repeat the numbers 60 through 100.

Numbers 60–100

60	soixante	78	soixante-dix-huit
70	soixante-dix	79	soixante-dix-neuf
71	soixante et onze	80	quatre-vingts
72	soixante-douze	81	quatre-vingt-un
73	soixante-treize	90	quatre-vingt-dix
74	soixante-quatorze	91	quatre-vingt-onze
75	soixante-quinze	99	quatre-vingt-dix-neuf
76	soixante-seize	100	cent
77	soixante-dix-sept		

Spell out the numbers below and practice saying them aloud.

Ça coûte combien, le champagne?
Le Bollinger coûte …

How much does the champagne cost?
The Bollinger costs …

7. *Listen to find out which is the right bill for each table.*

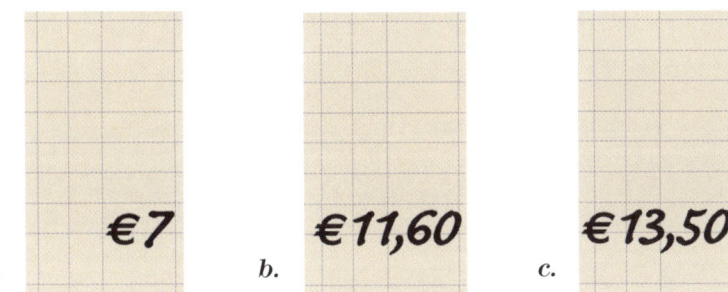

a. €7   b. €11,60   c. €13,50

d. €13,70   e. €14,50

Pronunciation

Rappel! *More practice with* **un** *and* **une**. *Remember* **un** *is used with masculine words and* **une** *is used with feminine words.*

Listen and repeat these phrases:

un verre de vin rouge

un café

un sandwich au jambon

une tarte aux pommes

une glace au chocolat

une omelette aux fines herbes

Close-up

Rappel! The word for "the" with masculine words is **le** and with feminine words it is **la**. The word for "a" with masculine words is **un** and with feminine words it is **une**. The plural forms for both m. and f. are **les** (the) and **des** (some).

	m.	f.	pl.
the	**le** sandwich	**la** glace	**les** sandwichs, **les** glaces
a/some	**un** sandwich	**une** glace	**des** sandwichs, **des** glaces

When talking about flavors and fillings, you use **à + le/la/les**:

une glace **à la** vanille   a vanilla-flavored ice cream

Now see what happens to **à** in front of **le** and **les**:

	m.	f.	pl.
	à + le = **au**	à la	à + les = **aux**
	le chocolat	la vanille	les pistaches
une glace	**au** chocolat	**à la** vanille	**aux** pistaches

How would you ask for the following?

une tarte + le citron   une tarte + la fraise   une tarte + les pommes

Chez le marchand de journaux

At the newsstand

Word Bank

l'argent *m.*	*money*	le paquet de bonbons	*packet of candy*
la carte de téléphone	*telephone card*	le plan de la ville	*town plan*
la carte postale	*postcard*	le timbre (-poste)	*(postage) stamp*
le journal	*newspaper*	acheter	*to buy*
le magazine	*magazine*	coûter	*to cost*

1. *Mme Millerioux is buying a newspaper in Paris. Listen to find out what else she wants to buy.* **Le Figaro** *is a leading French newspaper.* **Télérama** *and* **Télépoche** *are television listings magazines.*

Je regrette …
I'm sorry …

Unit 2 **29**

2. *How much do the magazines cost? Listen and write down the prices.*

3. **Ça fait combien?** *Tell Mme Millerioux how much these journals cost.*

a. Le *New York Herald* coûte _____.

b. Le *London Times* coûte _____.

c. *Le Monde* coûte _____.

d. *Libération* coûte _____.

Did you get it right? Listen and find out.

Did You Know?

All euro coins have a common face and a national face specific to each member country. The French motto, "Liberté, Egalité, Fraternité" (Liberty, Equality, Brotherhood) is included on the one and two euro coins that are printed at the Paris Mint.

4. *Listen to Gilles and Sylvie buying some things at the same newsstand. Write down what they buy and how much they have to pay.*

Oui, bien sûr.	Yes, of course.
C'est tout?	Is that all?
C'est tout.	That's all.
Voilà.	There you are.

5. **A vous!** *How would you ask for these items?*

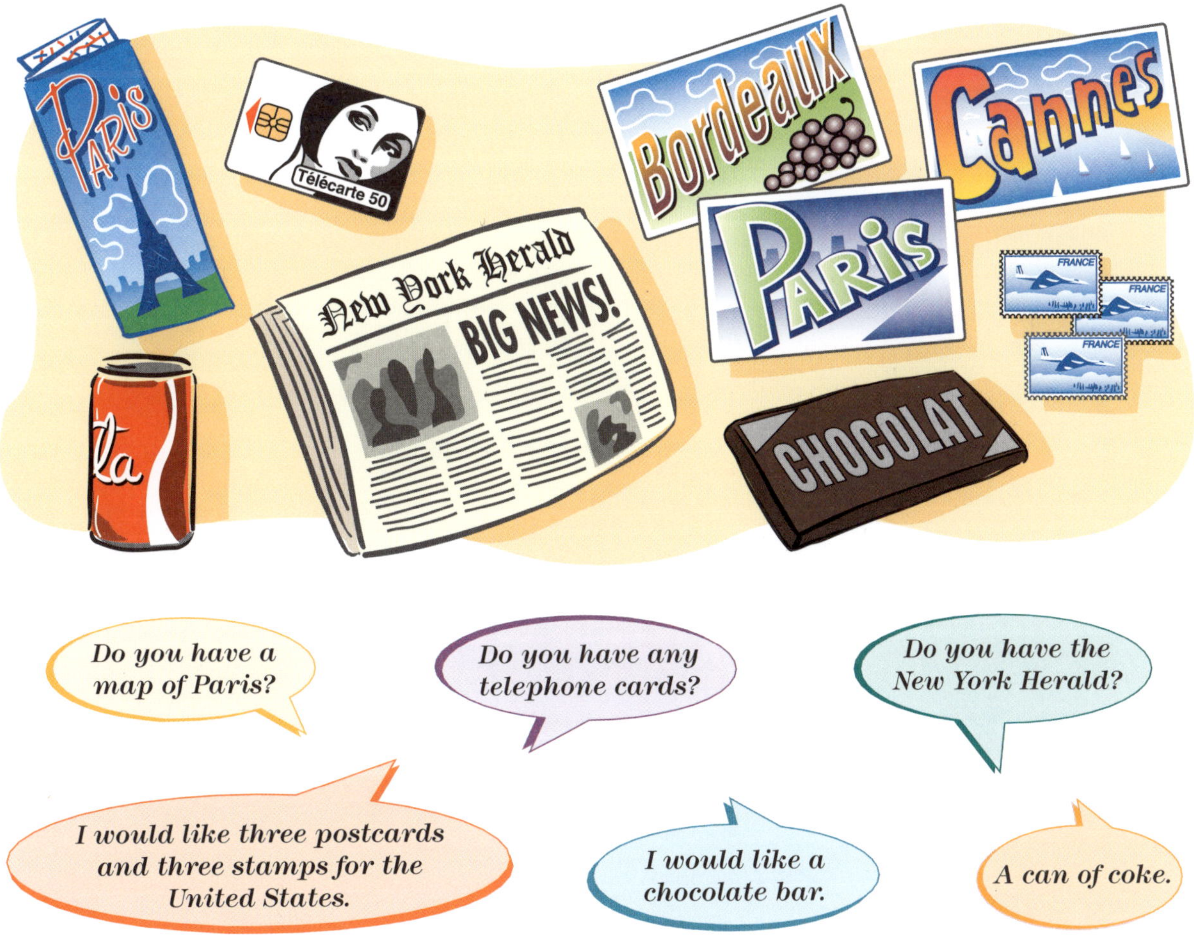

- Do you have a map of Paris?
- Do you have any telephone cards?
- Do you have the New York Herald?
- I would like three postcards and three stamps for the United States.
- I would like a chocolate bar.
- A can of coke.

Did you get it right? Listen and find out.

6. *How much do these items cost? Listen and find out.*

Learning tips

The numbers 60 through 100 are quite difficult to distinguish when spoken quickly. Pick out the ones that occur most frequently and practice saying them until you get used to the sound of them: 25, 50, 60, 75, 80, 95, 99.

Pronunciation

Listen and repeat these numbers:
25, 50, 60, 75, 80, 95, 99.

Now listen and practice the nasal "n" and "m" sounds:

un paquet de bonbons

des timbres

bien sûr

non

cent

Close-up

*If you are asking for one thing you use **un** or **une**:*
Avez-vous un paquet de bonbons/une carte postale?
Do you have a packet of candy/a postcard?

*If you are asking for some/any you use **des**:*
Avez-vous des cartes postales/des timbres?
Do you have any postcards/stamps?

Rappel! *All nouns in French are either masculine or feminine.*
The definite article ("the") and indefinite article ("a") have different forms in French depending on whether the noun is masculine or feminine:

With masculine words:	un café	*a coffee*	le café	*the coffee*
With feminine words:	une bière	*a beer*	la bière	*the beer*

*Use **l'** before words that begin with a vowel or "h":*

un hôtel	*a hotel*	l'hôtel	*the hotel*

*To make the plural, you usually add **s** to the end of the word, as in English:*

un crème	deux crèmes
un café	deux cafés

*But the **s** ending is not pronounced.*

Checkpoints

Use this checklist to test what you've learned in this unit and review anything you're not sure of.

Can you ... ?   Yes   No

- *order something to drink* .... ❏ .... ❏
  Je voudrais un café.
  Je voudrais un jus d'orange.

- *say you would like a large* .... ❏ .... ❏
  Je voudrais un grand café.

- *say you would like a small* .... ❏ .... ❏
  Je voudrais un petit café.

- *ask if they have something* .... ❏ .... ❏
  Avez-vous des croissants?

- *ask for the bill, please* .... ❏ .... ❏
  L'addition, s'il vous plaît.

- *ask what sort of sandwiches they have* .... ❏ .... ❏
  Qu'est-ce que vous avez comme sandwichs?

- *and what sort of ice cream* .... ❏ .... ❏
  Qu'est-ce que vous avez comme glaces?

- *order something to eat* .... ❏ .... ❏
  Je voudrais un sandwich au jambon.
  Je voudrais un steak frites.
  Pour moi, une salade niçoise.
  Pour moi, une tarte aux pommes.
  Pour moi, une glace au chocolat.

- *order a drink with your meal* .... ❏ .... ❏
  Une bière, s'il vous plaît.
  Un verre de vin rouge.
  De l'eau minérale (gazeuse ou non gazeuse).

- *say the numbers 20–100* .... ❏ .... ❏

- *ask how much something costs* .... ❏ .... ❏
  Ça coûte combien?

- *and say how much something costs* .... ❏ .... ❏
  Ça coûte …

Can you ... ?   Yes   No

- *ask for items* .... ☐ ..... ☐
  Avez vous une carte de téléphone?
  Avez vous des cartes postales?
  Avez vous un paquet de bonbons?
  Avez vous un plan de la ville?
  Avez-vous des timbres?

- *and say that's all* .... ☐ ..... ☐
  C'est tout.

- *say thank you* .... ☐ ..... ☐
  Merci monsieur/madame.

Learning tips

French words don't always sound the way they are written. When you read a French word, try to think of the way it sounds, and keep listening to the dialogs. You may find it helpful to write down how a word sounds to you, for example:
Avez-vous = "avay-voo," **huit** = "wheat," and so on.

When you ask a question in French you end the question on a rising note:

Avez-vous des cartes de téléphone?

Record yourself saying new words and phrases aloud. Play them back and compare your accent and intonation with those in the dialogs.

Do you want to learn more?

If someone you know is going to a French-speaking country, ask him or her to bring back magazines with cooking recipes and checks from restaurants and cafés. Some restaurants and cafés may let you take a menu. See how many names of foods and drinks you can identify, and practice ordering them.

For more practice, see Extra! on page A4.

Unit 3 concentrates on "small talk," conversational topics, and social chat. When you have completed the unit, you will know how to:

- talk about what you do and where you work
- talk about your own and ask about someone else's family
- talk about what you are going to do

Au travail et en famille 3

Word Bank

l'agent de police *m.*	*policeman/woman*
l'agent des postes *m.*	*post office worker*
l'artiste graphique *m. and f.*	*graphic artist*
l'avocat *m.*	*lawyer*
le/la comptable	*accountant*
le cuisinier/la cuisinière	*cook*
le dessinateur/la dessinatrice	*illustrator*
le directeur/la directrice	*director*
l'employé(e)	*employee*
l'étudiant(e)	*student*
l'informaticien(ne)	*computer technician*
l'infirmier/l'infirmière	*nurse*
l'instituteur/l'institutrice	*primary teacher*
le/la journaliste	*journalist*
le/la mécanicien(ne)	*mechanic*
le médecin	*doctor*
le métier	*job*
le professeur	*teacher*
le/la secrétaire	*secretary*
le/la scientifique	*scientist*
l'atelier *m.*	*workshop/studio*
la banque	*bank*
le bureau	*office*
le centre hospitalier	*hospital complex*
la clinique	*clinic*
le commissariat de police	*central police station*
l'entreprise *f.*	*business*
l'hôpital *m.*	*hospital*
le magasin	*shop*
le salon de coiffure	*hairdressing salon*
la bureautique	*office work*
le commerce	*commerce*
le droit	*law*
l'enseignement *m.*	*education*
l'hôtellerie *f.*	*hotel and catering*
l'informatique *f.*	*information technology*
les médias	*the media*
les postes et télécommunications	*post and telecommunications*
les ressources humaines	*human resources*
la santé	*health*
les sciences et techniques	*science and technology*
le secteur automobile	*the automobile industry*
dans	*in*
toujours	*still*
faire attention	*to be careful*

Quel est votre métier?

Talking about jobs

1. *Listen to the game show presenter asking contestants about their jobs. Check the words you hear him say in the list below. Notice that many words have a special form for the feminine.*

m.	f.	
l'agent de police	l'agent de police	*policeman/woman*
le coiffeur	la coiffeuse	*hairdresser*
le cuisinier	la cuisinière	*cook*
le directeur	la directrice	*director*
l'étudiant	l'étudiante	*student*
l'homme d'affaires	la femme d'affaires	*businessman/woman*
l'instituteur	l'institutrice	*primary teacher*
le médecin	le médecin	*doctor*
le vendeur	la vendeuse	*salesperson*

Quel est votre métier?	*What is your job?*
Que faites-vous dans la vie?	*What do you do for a living?*
Je suis au chômage.	*I am out of work.*
Je travaille à mon compte.	*I am self-employed.*
Je travaille à mi-temps.	*I work part time.*

Did You Know?

To know and understand the use of gestures—either to accompany or replace the spoken word—is to know an essential element of culture.

The French repertoire of gestures is extensive, varied and highly original. Learn to pay attention to body language and movement. For example, using an index finger to pull down the lower eyelid is to say, "Mon œil!" or My eye, literally, but figuratively, "I don't believe you!"

2. *Some people in your hotel are introducing themselves. Listen to them telling you about their jobs and where they work, then join their names to their job titles and workplaces.*

Gilles Bernard	dessinatrice de BD	une entreprise
Sylvie Verlaine	employé de banque	un atelier
Lucienne Briand	infirmière	un hôpital
Patrice Millerioux	directeur des ressources humaines	une banque

3. *These people want to join in the conversation but their French is not very good. Can you help them say what they do and where they work? First write down what you think they should say, then listen to Sylvie helping them.*

Carmen Fernandez	Paul Black	Isabella Rossi	Jack Nicholls
informaticienne	guide touristique	vendeuse	agent de police
une entreprise	un bureau de tourisme	un grand magasin	un commissariat de police

  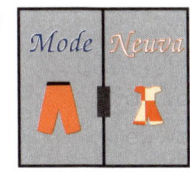 

a. Je suis _____ et je travaille dans _____.

b. Je suis _____ et je travaille dans _____.

c. Je suis _____ et je travaille dans _____.

d. Je suis _____ et je travaille dans _____.

4. *Now it's your turn to tell the others what you do. Answer the question by completing the following sentence, then practice saying it aloud.*

Que faites-vous?

Je suis _____ et je travaille _____.

5. (RECORDING) *See if you can introduce these people. Prepare your text first, then read it aloud, if possible into a tape-recorder so that you can listen to yourself speaking. Do you sound French? Now listen to the group leader M. Martin making the introductions. Note his intonation and see if you can copy it.*

a. M. Bernard, de Genève en Suisse. Il est _____ et travaille dans _____.

b. Mme Rossi, de Rome en Italie. Elle est _____ et travaille dans _____.

c. M. Nicholls, de New York. Il est _____ et travaille _____.

d. Mlle Verlaine, de Paris. Elle est _____ et travaille dans _____.

e. Mme Briand, de Bruxelles, en Belgique. Elle est _____ et travaille dans _____.

f. Mlle Fernandez, de Madrid, en Espagne. Elle est _____ et travaille dans _____.

g. M. Millerioux, de Québec, au Canada. Il est _____ et travaille dans _____.

h. M. Black, de Londres, en Angleterre. Il est _____ et travaille dans _____.

Je vous présente …	Let me introduce …
Voici …	Here is …
Il/elle est …	He/she is …
Il/elle travaille dans …	He/she works in …

6. *Match the job with the appropriate field.*

l'agent des postes	le secteur automobile
l'avocat	la bureautique
le/la comptable	le commerce
le cuisinier/la cuisinière	le droit
l'informaticien(ne)	l'enseignement
l'infirmier/l'infirmière	l'hôtellerie
le/la journaliste	l'informatique
le/la mécanicien(ne)	les médias
le professeur	les postes et télécommunications
le/la secrétaire	la santé
le/la scientifique	les sciences et techniques

Dans quel secteur travaillent-ils?   *Which field do they work in?*

7. *Which field do you work in? Write down your answer or, if you are not working at the moment, say what field you'd like to work in. Practice saying your answer aloud.*

Dans quel secteur travaillez-vous? Je travaille dans _____.

Dans quel secteur voulez-vous travailler? Je voudrais travailler dans _____.

Pronunciation

Listen and repeat the parts of the verbs **travailler** *and* **faire** *to get used to how they sound. Remember that all parts of an* **-er** *verb sound the same except the* **nous** *and* **vous** *forms.*

Unit 3   **41**

Close-up

Useful verbs

travail**ler**—*to work*

je travaill**e**	nous travaill**ons**
tu travaill**es**	vous travaill**ez**
il travaill**e**	ils travaill**ent**
elle travaill**e**	elles travaill**ent**

Travailler is a regular **-er** verb. Most verbs which end in **-er** take the same endings. All parts of the **-er** verb sound the same except the **nous** and **vous** forms.

*faire—*to do*

je fai**s**	nous fai**sons**
tu fai**s**	vous fai**tes**
il fai**t**	ils f**ont**
elle fai**t**	elles f**ont**

Faire is an irregular verb. You should learn the parts you are going to need most:

Que faites-vous?	What do you do?/What are you doing?
je fais	I do/I am doing
il/elle fait	(s)he does/is doing

Les métiers

Some words for jobs have a different form for the masculine and feminine.

a. Words ending in **é** add an **e**:

un employ**é** *m.* une employ**ée** *f.*

b. Words ending in **er** change to **ère**:

l'infirm**ier** *m.* l'infirm**ière** *f.*
le boulang**er** *m.* la boulang**ère** *f.*

c. Words ending in **en** change to **enne**:

le mécanic**ien** *m.* la mécanic**ienne** *f.*
l'électric**ien** *m.* l'électric**ienne** *f.*

d. Words ending in **eur**: change to **ice** or **euse**:

le fact**eur** *m.* la factr**ice** *f.*
le coiff**eur** *m.* la coiff**euse** *f.*

*Irregular verbs are indicated with an asterisk.

Une photo de ma famille

A photo of my family

1. *You are talking to some of the guests in the hotel lounge. Listen to each of them telling Sylvie how old they are and whether they are married or single. Beside each name below, write their age and the appropriate letter to indicate their marital status.*

C	**célibataire**	*single*
D	**divorcé(e)**	*divorced*
M	**marié(e)**	*married*
S	**séparé(e)**	*separated*

a. Gilles Bernard   *e.* Lucienne Briand

b. Isabella Rossi   *f.* Carmen Fernandez

c. Paul Black   *g.* Patrice Millerioux

d. Jack Nicholls   *h.* Sylvie Verlaine

Now you tell them about yourself:

J'ai _____ ans et je suis _____.

Quel âge avez-vous?   *How old are you?*
J'ai 32 ans.   *I'm 32.*

Word Bank

l'âge *m.*	age	le père	father
l'ami(e)	friend	la mère	mother
un(e) petit(e) ami(e)	a boyfriend/girlfriend	les parents	parents
		les grands-parents	grandparents
le mari	husband	le frère/le demi-frère	brother/half-brother
la femme	wife	la sœur/la demi-sœur	sister/half-sister
l'enfant *m.* and *f.*	child	Quel/Quelle?	What?
la fille	daughter	Que ... ?	What ... ?
le fils	son		

Unit 3

2. You are having a phone conversation with a French-speaking friend who's curious to know about the people in the group. Listen and answer her questions.

3. Patrice is showing you a photograph of his family. Listen and find out the names of the people in the photograph. Match the names with their relationship to Patrice.

| ma femme | ma mère | mon père | mon fils |
| ma fille | mon chien | moi | |

Murielle   Patrice   Véronique   Samuel

Didier   Jean-Claude   Elodie

à droite	on the right
à gauche	on the left
à côté de	beside (lit: on the side of)
entre	between
puis	then
me voilà	here I am

44 *French*

Now listen to Patrice telling you how old they are. Write each person's age in the box below his or her name.

Il a quel âge?	How old is he? (lit: He has what age?)
Elle a quel âge?	How old is she?
Ils/Elles ont quel âge?	How old are they?

Listen to Sylvie and Thierry talking about their family photos. Put an S beside the photos belonging to Sylvie and a T beside those belonging to Thierry. Write down in English who is in each picture.

a.

b.

c.

d.

en vacances	on vacation
au bord de la mer	at the seaside
à la maison	at home
devant la maison	in front of the house

6. *Now you are going to show some pictures of your family. See if you can find some real ones to talk about. Prepare what you are going to say in writing, taking care to use the right form of* **mon, ma,** *and* **mes.**

Voici _____ (mère). Elle s'appelle

_____ et elle a _____ ans.

Et voici _____ (père). Il s'appelle

_____ et il a _____ ans.

Voici _____ .

Pronunciation

When saying "p" and "t" keep your lips tighter than you do when speaking English. Listen and practice saying:
mon petit ami; ma petite amie; son petit ami; sa petite amie.

When asking a question in French notice how the voice rises at the end of the question, and when making a statement the voice falls at the end of the sentence. Listen carefully and repeat these phrases:

Ça va?

Ça va bien, merci.

Il a quel âge?

Il a vingt ans.

Avez-vous une photo de votre femme?

Oui, j'ai une photo de ma famille.

Close-up

Rappel! *All nouns in French are masculine or feminine. Like the words for "the" and "a," the words for "my," "his," and "her" also change to agree with the noun they precede.*

m.	<u>mon</u> mari	<u>son</u> fils
	my husband	his/her son
f.	<u>ma</u> femme	<u>sa</u> fille
	my wife	his/her daughter
pl.	<u>mes</u> enfants	<u>ses</u> parents
	my children	his/her parents

Before feminine nouns that begin with a vowel, you use **mon** *and* **son**:

<u>mon</u> ami—*my (male) friend*
<u>mon</u> amie—*my (female) friend*

<u>son</u> ami—*his/her (male) friend*
<u>son</u> amie—*his/her (female) friend*
and of course they both sound the same!

But if you want to say "my boyfriend" you say: **mon petit ami** *and "my girlfriend" is:* **ma petite amie**.

Qu'est-ce qu'on va faire?

What shall we do?

1. *In the hotel bar, Sylvie and Patrice are deciding what to do this evening. Listen to Sylvie's suggestions and tick the ones she mentions.*

Qu'est-ce qu'on va faire ce soir?	*What shall we do this evening?*
On pourrait aller …	*We could go …*
Je ne veux pas …	*I don't want to …*
le long de	*along*
ou bien	*or (indeed)*
Bonne idée!	*Good idea!*

2. *What does everyone decide to do? Listen to the conversation and match the names to the activities they've chosen.*

a.	Gilles Bernard	va aller au cinéma
b.	Mme Fourrier	va aller au lit
c.	M. Delafin	va rester au bar et boire une bière
d.	Sylvie Verlaine	va faire une promenade en ville
e.	Mme Coulot	va aller danser
f.	M. Garnier	va aller au restaurant
g.	Patrice Millerioux	va aller en boîte de nuit

Word Bank

le bar	bar	fatigué(e)	tired
la boîte (de nuit)	night club	*aller	to go
le cinéma	movies	*boire	to drink
le lit	bed	danser	to dance
le musée	museum	*faire une promenade	to go for a walk
la piscine	swimming pool	manger	to eat
le restaurant	restaurant	rester	to stay
le théâtre	theater	*venir	to come
le tour	tour	visiter	to visit
la ville	town		

3. Listen to the recording for activity 2 again. The tour guide, M. Martin, wants to know what everyone is going to do. Write down what you would say to tell him, then practice reading it aloud.

Gilles Bernard va _____.

Mme Fourrier _____.

M. Delafin _____.

Sylvie Verlaine _____.

Mme Coulot _____.

M. Garnier _____.

Patrice Millerioux _____.

4. Has M. Martin understood you correctly? Listen and answer his questions.

Oui, c'est vrai.	Yes, that's right.
Bonne soirée!	Have a nice evening!

Unit 3 **49**

5. *Now M. Martin is asking you what you are going to do. Complete the sentence and practice saying it aloud, then answer his questions.*

Et vous, qu'est-ce que vous allez faire?

Je vais …   I'm going to …

Je ne sais pas.   I don't know.

6. *Imagine the same people are staying in a hotel in your home town. Suggest three things they could do.*

On pourrait …

Pronunciation

The letters "n" and "m" preceded by a vowel are called nasal sounds because they are produced through the nose. Listen carefully to the pronunciation of **on** *and try to copy it as you repeat these phrases:*

On va danser.

On va au cinéma.

On va au restaurant.

On va en ville.

Close-up

More verbs

*aller—to go

je vais	nous allons
tu vas	vous allez
il va	ils vont
elle va	elles vont

Je vais can mean either "I go" or "I am going."

The "near future" tense

Aller *is also used, as in English, to translate the near future, I am going to:*

Je vais aller au cinéma.
I am going to go to the cinema.

Tu vas aller danser.
You are going to go dancing.

Il va aller à la piscine.
He is going to go to the swimming pool.

Elle va aller en ville.
She is going to go to town.

On va sortir.
We are going to go out. (lit: one is going to go out)

Nous allons boire une bière.
We are going to have a beer.

Vous allez faire une promenade.
You are going for a walk.

Ils/Elles vont visiter la ville.
They are going to see the sights. (lit: visit the town)

Checkpoints

Use the check list to test what you've learned in this unit and review anything you're not sure of.

Can you ... ?   Yes   No

- *say what job you do* .... ❑ ..... ❑
  Je suis employé(e) de banque/étudiant(e)/médecin

- *and where you work* .... ❑ ..... ❑
  Je travaille dans une banque/une société/un bureau

- *what someone else does* .... ❑ ..... ❑
  Il/elle est …

- *and where he/she works* .... ❑ ..... ❑
  Il/elle travaille dans …

- *in which field you work* .... ❑ ..... ❑
  Je travaille dans …

- *or would like to work* .... ❑ ..... ❑
  Je voudrais travailler …

- *say what your marital status is* .... ❑ ..... ❑
  Je suis célibataire/marié(e)/séparé(e)/divorcé(e)

- *who the members of your family are as if showing photos* .... ❑ ..... ❑
  Voici mon (père)/ma (mère)/mes (enfants)/mon (chien)

- *what they are called* .... ❑ ..... ❑
  Il/elle s'appelle …

- *and how old they are* .... ❑ ..... ❑
  Il/elle a … ans

- *talk about what you are going to do* .... ❑ ..... ❑
  Je vais aller danser.
  Je vais aller au cinéma.
  Je vais visiter la ville.
  Je vais aller manger.
  Je vais faire une promenade.
  Je vais aller au bar.

- *say what he/she is going to do* .... ❑ ..... ❑
  Il/elle va …

Can you ... ?   **Yes**   **No**

- **say what two or more are going to do** .... ☐ ...... ☐
  On va ...

- **suggest what you might do** .... ☐ ...... ☐
  On pourrait ...

- **say you don't know** .... ☐ ...... ☐
  Je ne sais pas.

Learning tip

Practice is very important when learning a language. Listen regularly to the recording and always say the French aloud when you are asked to speak. If you feel self-conscious try putting your hands over your ears. This will help you to hear your own voice better and you will not need to speak so loudly. If possible record some sentences and play them back to hear how you sound, but don't be discouraged—everybody thinks they sound awful!

Do you want to learn more?

Turn to the employment advertisements in a French-language newspaper to see how many of the jobs you recognize. Use clues from the name of the company. Guess what the job title might mean, and check with your dictionary.

For more practice, see Extra! on page A7.

Unit 4 will help you learn the language you need to find your way around a town. By the end, you will know how to:

- find out where a place is
- ask for and give directions to a place
- ask about opening and closing times

En ville

4

Word Bank

l'arrêt d'autobus *m.*	bus stop
la banque	bank
le bus	bus
le car	coach, bus
l'église *f.*	church
la gare	train station
le parking	parking lot/car park
la place du marché	marketplace
la pharmacie	pharmacy
la poste	post office
la rue	street
la station de métro	subway station
la station-service	gas station
la station de taxi	taxi stand
le supermarché	supermarket
le taxi	taxi
à côté de	beside/next to
à droite	to the right
à gauche	to the left
au coin de	on the corner
derrière	behind
devant	in front of
en face de	opposite
ici	here
là-bas	over there
où?	where?
sur	on
changer de l'argent	to change money
*prendre	to take
SNCF (la Société nationale des chemins de fer)	French National Railways

Il y a une banque près d'ici?

Is there a bank near here?

RECORDING 1. Listen to these people at the hotel reception desk. Check the symbols below if the clerk says there is one nearby, and put a cross if there isn't.

La gare SNCF est près d'ici?	Is the train station near here?
(C'est) à deux minutes.	(It's) only two minutes away.
Il faut aller au centre-ville.	You have to go downtown.
Il faut prendre le bus/ le métro/un taxi.	You have to take the bus/subway/ a taxi.
Il y a un bus toutes les dix minutes.	There is a bus every ten minutes.

RECORDING 2. *Listen to these people asking where the nearest subway station is and choose the right sketch.*

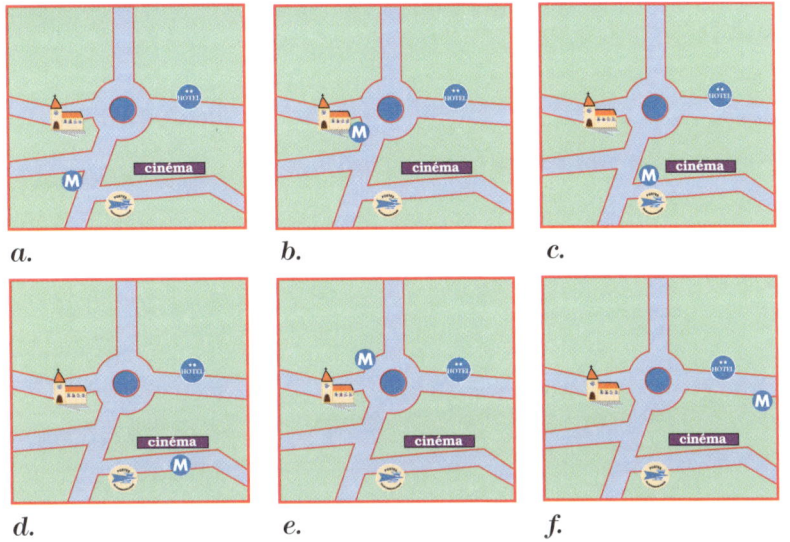

a. b. c.

d. e. f.

C'est tout près.
It's quite near.

sur votre droite
on your right

sur votre gauche
on your left

RECORDING 3. *The clerk is telling some hotel guests where to find certain places. Listen to the recording. Look at the list of places. Then put them in their proper location on the map.*

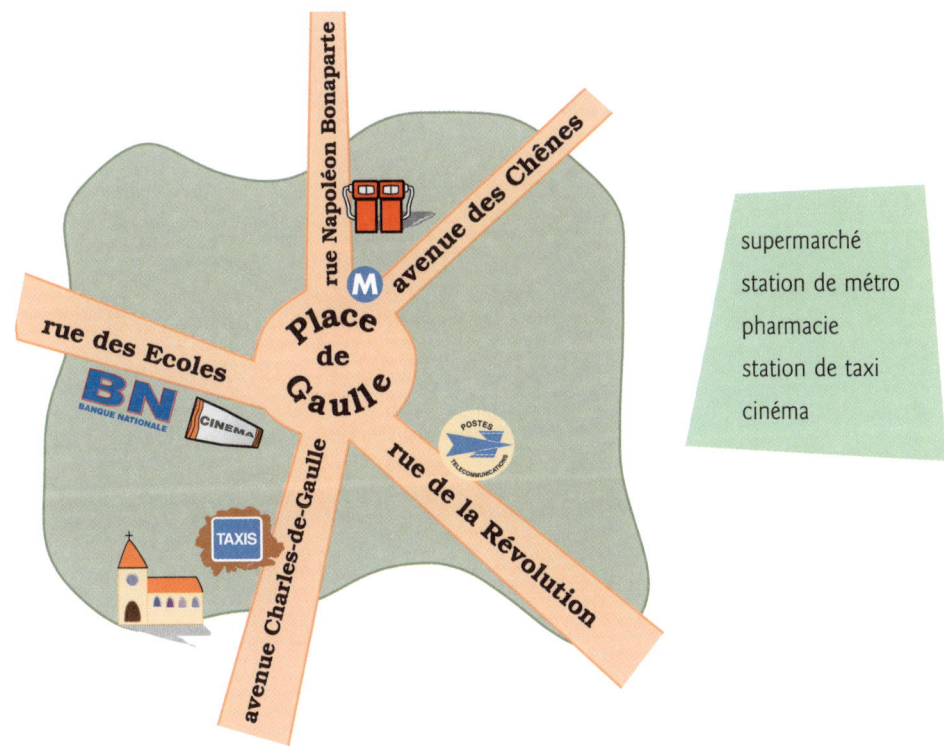

supermarché
station de métro
pharmacie
station de taxi
cinéma

Unit 4

4. Now some other people are asking you where these places are. Look at the map again and see if you can help them. Complete the conversations below and then listen again to check your answers.

   a. Est-ce qu'il y a une banque près d'ici?_____.
   b. Il y a une station-service près d'ici? _____.
   c. Il y a une pharmacie près d'ici? _____.
   d. Est-ce qu'il y a une station de taxi près d'ici? _____.
   e. Est-ce qu'il y a une station de métro près d'ici? _____.

5. You are visiting Lucienne in Belgium. From her answers below, can you work out what questions you might have asked her?

   a. La gare? Il n'y a pas de gare ici.
   b. La piscine? Ah non, il faut prendre le bus.
   c. La poste? Tout près, à gauche.
   d. Pour une pharmacie? Il faut aller en ville.
   e. Le cinéma est en face de l'hôtel.

6. Now Lucienne is visiting you and has asked you the same questions. How would you answer them? Write out what you would say, then practice saying it aloud.

Pronunciation

Here's more practice at making statements and asking questions. Listen and repeat these phrases, paying particular attention to the intonation:

Il y a une piscine près d'ici?

Il y a une piscine près d'ici.

La banque est près d'ici?

La banque est près d'ici.

La pharmacie est en face de l'hôtel?

La pharmacie est en face de l'hôtel.

Now practice using **Est-ce que**:

Est-ce qu'il y a une piscine près d'ici?

Est-ce qu'il y a une banque près d'ici?

Est-ce qu'il y a une pharmacie près d'ici?

Est-ce qu'il y a une station de métro près d'ici?

Close-up

To ask a question the easiest way is to say the statement with a rising tone:

Il y a une banque près d'ici?	Is there a bank near here?
Oui, il y a une banque à gauche.	Yes, there's a bank on the left.

Another way is to precede the statement with **Est-ce que** *(lit: Is it that ... ?).*

Note that the **que** *becomes* **qu'** *before a vowel:*

Est-ce qu'il y a une banque près d'ici?

Rappel! *To make a negative statement in French you add* **ne** *(or* **n'** *before a vowel) in front of the verb and* **pas** *after the verb:*

Non, il ne va pas au cinéma.

In French, when you say there isn't something, you add **de** *(of/any) after the negative and leave out the word for "the" or "a":*

Ah non, il n'y a pas de cinéma.	No, there isn't (any) movie theater.
Je n'ai pas de femme.	I don't have (a) wife.
Il n'y a pas de croissants.	There aren't any croissants.

Il faut

Il faut *is a useful impersonal phrase meaning "it is necessary to ... ," "you have to ... ":*

Il faut aller au centre-ville.	You have to go downtown.
Il faut prendre le bus.	You have to take the bus.

Pour aller à ... ?

How do you get to ... ?

 **1.** *Listen to these people asking the way and check the places they want to go.*

Excusez-moi ...   *Excuse me ...*

 **2.** **A vous!** *Now it's your turn to ask the way. Listen and answer the questions.*

Word Bank

l'aéroport *m.*	*airport*	le syndicat d'initiative	*tourist information office*
l'autoroute *f.*	*highway*	avant	*before*
la cathédrale	*cathedral*	mais	*but*
la gare routière	*bus station*	continuer	*to continue*
l'hypermarché *m.*	*large supermarket*	descendre	*to go down*
la plage	*beach*	monter	*to climb, go up*
la rue piétonne	*sidewalk*	traverser	*to cross*

3. *Which way should these people go? Listen to the directions and choose the right sketch.*

Rappel! *Don't forget that the French drive on the right the way Americans do.*

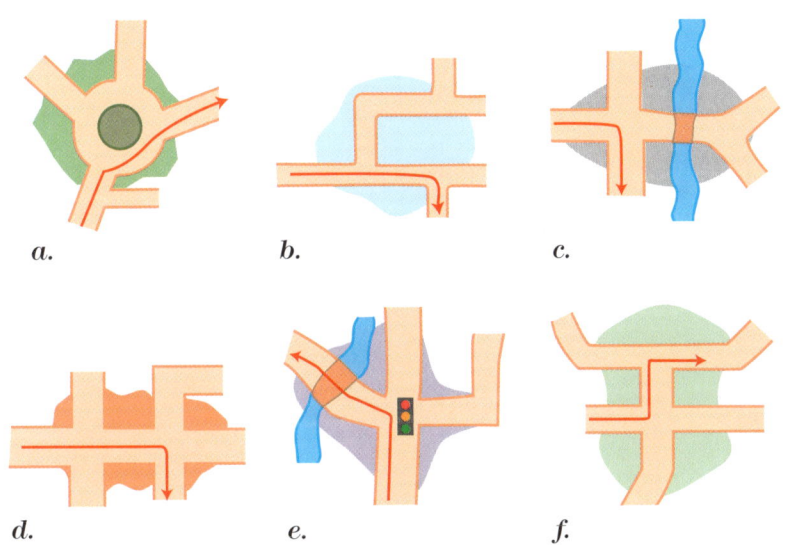

a.   b.   c.

d.   e.   f.

Vous allez tout droit.	You go straight ahead.
Vous tournez à droite.	You turn right.
Vous tournez à gauche.	You turn left.
Vous prenez la première rue à droite/gauche.	You take the first street on the right/left.
Vous prenez la deuxième rue à droite/gauche.	You take the second street on the right/left.
Vous traversez le pont.	You cross the bridge.
Vous montez/descendez en ville.	You go up/down into town.
jusqu'aux feux	to the lights
au rond-point	to the traffic circle

4. **A vous!** *Look at the sketches again and try to give the same directions. Prepare what you would say first, listen again to check, then practice reading them aloud.*

5. *First fill in the blanks below using the correct form of* **à la**, **au**, *or* **à l'**, *then listen to see if you got it right.*

a. _____ banque   e. _____ syndicat d'initiative
b. _____ aéroport   f. _____ musée
c. _____ poste   g. _____ hôtel
d. _____ hôpital   h. _____ plage

Now use these phrases to make complete sentences as if you were asking directions. Practice saying them aloud.

Example: Excusez-moi, pour aller à la banque, s'il vous plaît?

6. *Today you have a day off in Paris. Choose five places you would like to visit. How would you ask for directions? Be sure to use the right prepositions.*

la tour Eiffel	le Louvre
le musée d'Art moderne	la cathédrale Notre-Dame
la gare de Lyon	le Sacré-Cœur
la Seine	l'Arc de Triomphe
les Champs-Elysées	le jardin des Tuileries

Pronunciation

Listen and repeat these directions to get used to the sound of the **vous** *form of the verb:*

Vous prenez la première rue à gauche.

Vous allez jusqu'aux feux.

Vous tournez à gauche.

Vous traversez le pont.

Vous continuez tout droit.

Vous montez la rue.

Vous descendez la rue piétonne.

Now practice asking the way to these places in Paris:

à la place de la Concorde

à l'Etoile

au Centre Georges Pompidou

aux Halles

Close-up

When giving directions you use the **vous** form of the verb. The **vous** form of the verb ends in **-ez**. You have already used the **vous** form when asking questions:

<u>Parlez-vous</u> anglais?

<u>Avez-vous</u> des sandwichs?

<u>Êtes-vous</u> marié?

and in giving instructions:

<u>Parlez</u> plus lentement, s'il vous plaît.

When telling someone not to do something you use the usual **ne** (verb) **pas** construction:

Vous <u>ne</u> traversez <u>pas</u> le pont.   You don't cross the bridge.

Rappel!

à + la = <u>à la</u>	Pour aller <u>à la</u> place de la Concorde?
à + l' = <u>à l'</u>	Pour aller <u>à l'</u>Etoile?
à + le = <u>au</u>	Pour aller <u>au</u> Centre Georges Pompidou?
à + les = <u>aux</u>	Pour aller <u>aux</u> Halles?

Vous fermez à quelle heure?

What time do you close?

Véronique is asking at the hotel reception desk about opening times. Listen and write down the days when these places are open.

Ça ouvre à quelle heure?	What time does it open?
les heures d'ouverture	opening times
la fermeture de midi	midday closing
les jours de congés	days off
C'est ouvert …	It is open …
C'est fermé …	It is closed …
tous les jours	every day (lit: all the days)

DidYouKnow?

Most shops in France open at 9:00 and close at 18:30, but many shops, banks, and post offices close for lunch between 12:00 or 12:30 and 14:00. Most small food shops stay open later in the evening, some until about 20:00. The **boulangerie**, **pâtisserie**, and **fleuriste** are usually open on Sunday morning so that others can enjoy fresh bread and pastries, cakes, and flowers on their day off. Many shops, including some **boulangeries**, are closed on Monday morning.

64 French

Word Bank

les jours de la semaine	the days of the week	demain	tomorrow
		le matin	the morning
lundi	Monday	l'après-midi	the afternoon
mardi	Tuesday	le soir	the evening
mercredi	Wednesday	midi	midday
jeudi	Thursday	minuit	midnight
vendredi	Friday	sauf	except
samedi	Saturday	fermer	to close
dimanche	Sunday	ouvrir	to open
aujourd'hui	today		

RECORDING 2. Now listen again and choose the correct opening and closing times for each place.

Il/elle ouvre à …   It opens at …

Il/elle ferme à …   It closes at …

RECORDING 3. Lucienne is asking the hotel clerk about places where you can eat tonight. Listen and write down when they are open.

Unit 4

4. *You're more interested in going to the movies this evening. There is an English-language cinema downtown, so listen to find out what times the films are showing.*

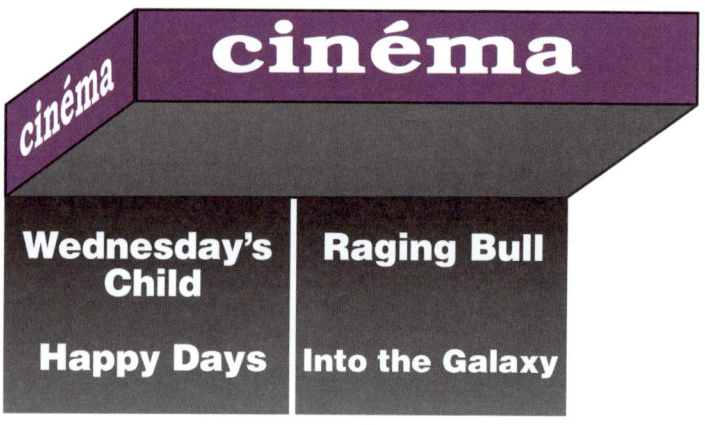

la salle   room (also used for screen in a multi-cinema complex)

5. *You have decided you really must get your hair done. Listen first and write down what times are available, then tell the hairdresser when you want to go.*

Now the others want you to make their appointments for them. Listen and tell the hairdresser when they want to go using **veut venir**.

Example: Mme Millerioux veut venir aujourd'hui à onze heures quarante-cinq.

Vous pouvez avoir rendez-vous à …	You can have an appointment at …
ou bien	or (indeed)
Je veux venir à …	I want to come at …

6. *Carmen would like to go to the Musée des Beaux-Arts. Tell her when it's open and write it down.*

Pronunciation

Rappel! *Here are pairs of words that are pronounced as one. Listen and repeat these times:*

une heure	sept heures
deux heures	huit heures
trois heures	neuf heures
quatre heures	dix heures
cinq heures	onze heures
six heures	douze heures

Close-up

Telling the time

Quelle heure est-il?	What time is it?
Il est une heure.	Il est deux heures moins le quart.
Il est une heure et demie.	Il est trois heures dix.
Il est huit heures cinq.	Il est trois heures moins dix.
Il est huit heures moins cinq.	Il est quatre heures vingt.
Il est deux heures et quart.	Il est quatre heures moins vingt.

In France the 24-hour clock is often used, especially when talking about opening and closing times.

14:30	quatorze heures trente
17:45	dix-sept heures quarante-cinq
19:55	dix-neuf heures cinquante-cinq
22:10	vingt-deux heures dix

Rappel! *In French all nouns are masculine or feminine. The word for "it" is* **il** *for masculine nouns,* **elle** *for feminine nouns:*

<u>Le cinéma</u> *ouvre à dix-huit heures?*   *Oui,* <u>il</u> *ouvre à dix-huit heures.*
Does the cinema open at 18:00?   *Yes, it opens at 18:00.*

<u>La banque</u> *ferme à quatorze heures?*   *Non,* <u>elle</u> *ne ferme pas à quatorze heures.*
Does the bank close at 14:00?   *No, it doesn't close at 14:00.*

Checkpoints

Use the check list to test what you've learned in this unit and review anything you're not sure of.

Can you ... ? Yes No

- *ask if there is a bank near the hotel* .... ❑ .... ❑
  Il y a une banque près de l'hôtel?

- *and say there is* .... ❑ .... ❑
  Il y a une banque près de l'hôtel.

- *and there isn't* .... ❑ .... ❑
  Il n'y a pas de banque.

- *say where something is* .... ❑ .... ❑
  en face de l'hôtel
  à côté de l'hôtel
  devant l'hôtel
  à gauche
  à droite

- *ask for directions* .... ❑ .... ❑
  Pour aller au restaurant?
  Pour aller à la gare?
  Pour aller à l'hôpital?
  Pour aller aux Champs-Elysées?

- *tell someone to turn right/left* .... ❑ .... ❑
  Vous tournez à droite/gauche.

- *tell someone to go straight ahead* .... ❑ .... ❑
  Vous allez tout droit.

- *tell someone not to cross the bridge* .... ❑ .... ❑
  Vous ne traversez pas le pont.

- *say the days of the week* .... ❑ .... ❑

- *give opening times* .... ❑ .... ❑
  Il/elle ouvre à ... heures et ferme à ... heures.

Learning tips

While you're out driving, cycling, or taking the dog for a walk, think about the directions you are taking. Tell yourself where to go (e.g., turn left, go straight ahead) in French.

Do you want to learn more?

When you're in France pick up hotel brochures. These often give written instructions as well as maps showing how to get there. See how many of the instructions you recognize. At home, collect brochures of tourist attractions near you and see if you could tell a French-speaking visitor about the opening hours.

For more practice, see Extra! on page A9.

Au centre commercial 5

Word Bank

la lotion après-rasage	aftershave
l'après-shampooing	conditioner
la boîte	box
la brosse	hairbrush
la brosse à dents	toothbrush
la crème hydratante	moisturizing cream
le dentifrice	toothpaste
le déodorant	deodorant
à bille	roll-on
en spray	spray
les kleenex *m. pl.*	tissues
le lait bronzant	sun cream
les lunettes de soleil *f. pl.*	sunglasses
le mouchoir en papier	paper handkerchief
le peigne	comb
le pharmacien/la pharmacienne	pharmacist
le rasoir	razor
le savon	soap
le sèche-cheveux (de voyage)	(travel) hair dryer
les serviettes hygiéniques *f. pl.*	sanitary napkins
le shampooing	shampoo
pour les cheveux fins	for fine hair
pour les cheveux normaux	for normal hair
les tampons	tampons
la trousse	toiletry bag
apporter	to bring
avoir besoin de	to need
oublier	to forget
préférer	to prefer

 la pharmacie

At the drugstore

1. *Listen and check the items these people say they have forgotten to bring.*

J'ai oublié mon/ma/mes ...	I have forgotten my ...
Ils ont oublié ...	They have forgotten ...
Il faut que j'achète ...	I must buy ...

 **2.** *Now listen to them buying the things they need and fill in the price tags.*

3. **A vous!** *Now say what you have forgotten. Write a list and practice reading it aloud, then listen to Sylvie.*

Example: J'ai oublié mon déodorant.

4. *Complete the dialog using* **je voudrais,** *I would like.*

Pharmacist: Vous désirez?

You: Je voudrais _____ déodorant.

Pharmacist: En bille ou en spray?

You: _____.

Pharmacist: Et avec ça?

You: _____ shampooing.

Pharmacist: Quelle sorte préférez-vous? Pour les cheveux fins ou normaux?

You: _____.

Pharmacist: Et de l'après-shampooing?

You: _____.

Pharmacist: C'est tout?

You: Non, avez-vous _____ dentifrice?

Pharmacist: Bien sûr, quelle marque?

You: "Signal" et des _____.

Pharmacist: Un paquet ou une boîte?

You: _____.

5. *Practice the dialog again, and tell the pharmacist what you want.*

Unit 5

Pronunciation

RECORDING

Rappel! *Do not sound the* **s** *or the* **t** *at the end of a word, as in* un paquet, le lait bronzant, la lotion après-rasage.

Practice saying these phrases:

un tube de dentifrice

une bouteille de shampooing

un paquet de kleenex

une boîte de mouchoirs en papier

Close-up

De

Notice the use of **de**, *meaning "of," in these expressions:*

un tube de dentifrice
a tube of toothpaste

une bouteille de shampooing
a bottle of shampoo

un paquet de kleenex
a packet of tissues

une boîte de mouchoirs en papier
a box of tissues

To say "some" you use **de + le/la/les**

m.	f.	pl.
(de + le) = du	de la	(de + les) = des
du shampooing	de la crème	des kleenex

If the noun begins with a vowel, use **de l'**:

de l'après-shampooing *m.*   de l'eau *f.*

French

Vous désirez?

Can I help you?

Word Bank

French	English	French	English
les bas *m.pl.*	stockings	la veste	jacket
le chemisier	blouse	les vêtements *m.pl.*	clothes
la casquette	cap	à carreaux	checked
le chapeau	hat	grand(e)	big
les chaussettes *f.pl.*	socks	petit(e)	small
les chaussures *f.pl.*	shoes	moyen(ne)	medium
la chemise	shirt	rayé(e)	striped
l'écharpe *f.*	scarf	beige	beige
les gants *f.pl.*	gloves	blanc(he)	white
la jupe	skirt	bleu(e)	blue
le manteau	coat	bleu marine	navy blue
le pantalon	pair of trousers	gris(e)	grey
le pull	sweater	jaune	yellow
la robe	dress	marron	brown
les sous-vêtements	underwear	noir(e)	black
le soutien-gorge	bra	rose	pink
le sweat-shirt	sweatshirt	rouge	red
la taille	size	vert(e)	green
le tee-shirt	T-shirt	chercher	to look for

1. *Listen to these six customers shopping for clothes and write down what they want.*

Qu'est-ce qu'ils cherchent?   *What are they looking for?*

Unit 5

2. *Now listen again and check which sizes they want.*

Quelle taille?   What size?

3. *Listen and check which item each customer prefers, (a) or (b). What do they say about their chosen item?*

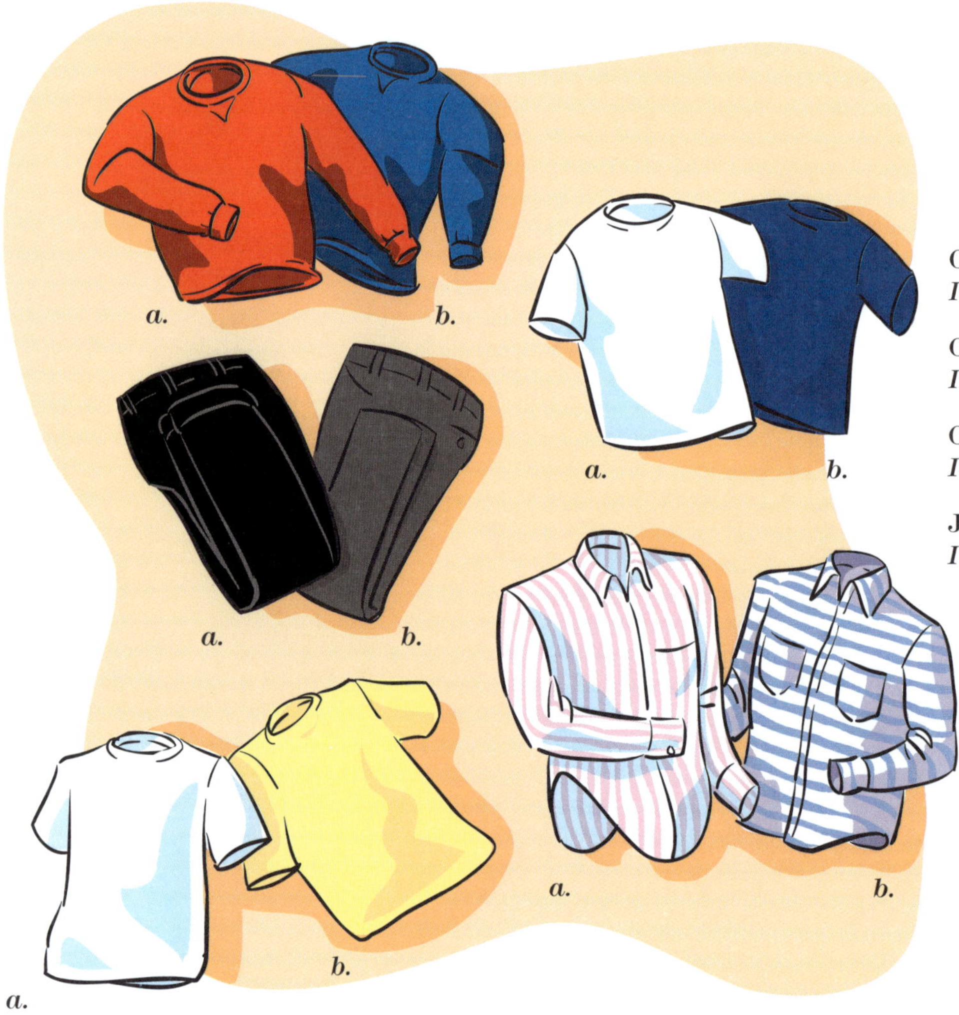

C'est chouette!
It's great.

C'est chic!
It's smart.

C'est branché!
It's trendy.

J'aime la couleur.
I like the color.

4. **À vous!** *Now you choose one item from each pair and write a list. Say what you think of your chosen item.*

Qu'est-ce que vous préférez?

Je préfère _____. C'est _____!

5. *Choose something you'd like to buy and then complete the dialog. Practice saying it out loud.*

> *Vendeuse:* Vous désirez?
>
> *You:* Je voudrais _____.
>
> *Vendeuse:* Quelle taille?
>
> *You:* _____.
>
> *Vendeuse:* Quelle couleur?
>
> *You:* _____.
>
> *Vendeuse:* Voilà! C'est tout?
>
> *You:* Oui, c'est tout.

6. *Now practice the dialog again, telling the salesperson what you would like when she asks you.*

Je regrette.	I'm sorry.
Je n'ai rien dans votre taille.	I have nothing in your size.

Pronunciation

Rappel! *Some letters at the end of a word are not usually sounded. However, when the feminine* **e** *is added, the letters* **d**, **t**, *and* **s** *are sounded. Listen to the difference in pronunciation between the masculine and feminine forms of these adjectives and then repeat each one:*

grand	grande
petit	petite
blanc	blanche
gris	grise
vert	verte

Adjectives of color come after the noun. Listen and repeat these phrases to get used to saying the adjective after the noun:

un pantalon blanc

une robe blanche

des pantalons blancs

des robes blanches

une veste bleue

une chemise rouge

un pantalon noir

des chaussettes grises

Close-up

Adjectives

Rappel! *All nouns in French are masculine or feminine.*

In French the adjective always agrees with the noun it describes. Most adjectives add an **e** *if the noun is feminine and an* **s** *if it is plural. Most adjectives come after the noun.*

m.	f.	m. pl.	f. pl.
un pantalon <u>noir</u>	une robe <u>noire</u>	des pantalons <u>noirs</u>	des robes <u>noires</u>

Le pantalon is a singular noun in French.

Some adjectives already end in **e** and don't change for the feminine form. They add an **s** for the plural:

un pantalon <u>rouge</u>	une robe <u>rouge</u>	des pantalons <u>rouges</u>	des robes <u>rouges</u>

The word for white—**blanc**—adds an **h** before the **e**. To help you remember think of the girl's name, Blanche:

un pantalon <u>blanc</u>	une robe <u>blanche</u>	des pantalons <u>blancs</u>	des robes <u>blanches</u>

Some common adjectives come in front of the noun, e.g., **petit(e)**, small, **grand(e)**, large:

une <u>petite</u> robe noire	*a little black dress*
un <u>grand</u> pantalon à carreaux	*a pair of large checked pants*

French

À la caisse

At the cash desk

Word Bank

la carte de crédit	*credit card*	écossais	*tartan (Scottish), plaid*
la carte bancaire	*banker's card*	combien ... ?	*how much ... ?*
le chèque	*check*	parce que	*because*
le chèque de voyage	*traveler's check*	trop	*too*
les espèces *f.pl.*	*cash*	long/longue	*long*
la cravate	*tie*	court/courte	*short*
en soie	*(in) silk*	large	*wide*
en cuir	*(in) leather*	cher/chère	*expensive*
en coton	*(in) cotton*	coûter	*to cost*
en laine	*(in) wool*	payer	*to pay*
le jean	*jeans*	signer	*to sign*

1. *Listen to some people making a purchase. How is each one paying? Match each conversation with the appropriate picture, then practice saying how you are going to pay.*

  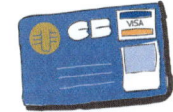 

Unit 5

Vous payez comment?
How are you going to pay?

en espèces
by cash

Vous avez une carte bancaire?
Do you have a banker's card?

Tapez votre numéro.
Type in your number.

Signez ici.
Sign here.

Did You Know?

In France credit cards contain a microchip. People paying by credit card are asked to type their personal identification number on a small keyboard to activate the chip and validate the card. If you do not have a French-style credit card you may be asked for additional identification.

RECORDING 2.

Listen to these prices and join each tie with its correct price. Listen again to check your answers.

RECORDING 3.

Listen to the dialog to find out how much these items cost, then fill in the price tags. Practice what you would say to tell a French visitor how much each item costs.

80 French

Ça coûte combien?
How much does it cost?

4. *Sylvie is helping you buy some presents. She points out the differences in price. Listen to what she says and complete the sentences below, then listen again to check your answers.*

Example: L'écharpe en soie grise est plus chère que l'écharpe en laine rouge.

a. L'écharpe en _____ est _____ que l'écharpe en laine.

b. La chemise en _____ est _____ que la chemise en soie.

c. Les gants en _____ sont _____ que les gants en laine.

d. La cravate en _____ est _____ que la cravate en soie rose.

e. Le pull en _____ est _____ que le pull en coton.

plus cher(s)/chère(s) (que)
more expensive (than)

moins cher(s)/chère(s) (que)
less expensive (than)

5. *You're looking at some more items with Sylvie and she tells you what she thinks of them. Listen and match the garment with the phrase she uses to describe it.*

la jupe	trop long(ue)
le pantalon	trop court(e)
le jean	trop large
le pull	trop cher/chère

6. *Listen to the dialogs, then match the questions with the correct answer.*

a. Vous voulez payer comment? Quarante.

b. Je peux payer avec une carte de crédit? Non, je regrette, pas en bleu marine.

c. Avez-vous ce pull en bleu marine? Noir.

d. Vous faites quelle taille? Non, je regrette, on n'accepte pas les cartes.

e. Quelle couleur voulez-vous? Avec un chèque de voyage.

Now it's your turn to be the customer. Listen and answer the salesperson's questions.

ce pull
this sweater

Pronunciation

Listen and repeat these phrases. Notice the difference in pronunciation between the masculine and feminine forms of the adjective.

Le pull. Il est trop long.

Le pantalon. Il est trop cher.

Le manteau. Il est trop court.

La chemise. Elle est trop longue.

La robe. Elle est trop chère.

La veste. Elle est trop courte.

Close-up

Rappel! *All nouns are masculine and feminine. To say "it" you use* **il** *for masculine nouns and* **elle** *for feminine nouns. With feminine nouns the adjectives must have feminine endings.*

m.	f.
Le pantalon bleu.	La veste noire.
Il est trop grand.	Elle est trop grande.

To say what something is made of, you use **en**:

| la veste en cuir | the leather jacket |
| le pantalon en laine | the woolen pants |

Unit 5

Checkpoints

Use the check list to test what you've learned in this unit and review anything you're not sure of.

Can you ... ?   Yes   No

- **ask for items at the pharmacy** .... ☐ ..... ☐
  un tube de dentifrice
  une bouteille de shampooing
  un paquet de kleenex
  une boîte de mouchoirs en papier

- **say you want a toothbrush** .... ☐ ..... ☐
  Je voudrais une brosse à dents.

- **say what you have forgotten** .... ☐ ..... ☐
  J'ai oublié mon/ma/mes ...

- **ask how much something costs** .... ☐ ..... ☐
  Ça coûte combien?

- **say you want (to buy) a sweater** .... ☐ ..... ☐
  Je voudrais (acheter) un pull.

- **say what size** .... ☐ ..... ☐
  taille ...

- **say what color** .... ☐ ..... ☐
  un pull bleu/vert/noir/rouge

- **say it's nice** .... ☐ ..... ☐
  C'est chouette!

- **say it's smart** .... ☐ ..... ☐
  C'est chic!

- **say it's trendy** .... ☐ ..... ☐
  C'est branché!

- **say you like the color** .... ☐ ..... ☐
  J'aime la couleur.

- **say how you are going to pay** .... ☐ ..... ☐
  avec une carte de crédit
  avec une carte bancaire
  avec un chèque de voyage
  avec un chèque
  en espèces

French

Can you ... ?   Yes   No

- *ask how much something is* .... ☐ ...... ☐
  C'est combien?

- *say what something is made of* .... ☐ ...... ☐
  en coton
  en laine
  en soie
  en cuir

- *make comparisons* .... ☐ ...... ☐
  plus cher/chère
  moins cher/chère
  trop cher/chère
  trop grand(e)/petit(e)/court(e)

Learning tips

French numbers can be difficult to distinguish when spoken quickly. The numbers 70 through 90 are usually the most difficult. Practice saying the numbers aloud and try to learn the sound of them.

Listen regularly to the dialogs and try to practice speaking French with other learners or French speakers. Find out about French societies or French programs on television or on the Internet. Buy a French magazine or look at one in a library, and see how many words you can already understand.

Do you want to learn more?

The ability to recognize cognates, or words that have a common original form, will measurably improve your reading skills and help you develop a more extensive vocabulary. You can begin by learning the following French suffixes and their English-language equivalents:

	French		**English**	
té	liber**té**	**ty**	liber**ty**	
	fratern**ité**		fratern**ity**	
ment	seule**ment**	**ly**	on**ly**	
	heureuse**ment**		fortunate**ly**	

For more practice, see Extra! on page A10.

Unit 5

Les moyens de transport 6

Word Bank

la banlieue	suburbs	en vélo	by bike
le car de ramassage	school bus	en voiture	by car
le collège	middle school	y	there
le métro	subway	arriver	to arrive
la moto	motorbike	conduire	to drive
la station	station	durer	to last
le train	train	faire un sondage	to conduct a survey
le travail	work	*prendre	to take
le vélo	bike	quitter	to leave (the house)
la voiture	car	sortir	to leave, go out
le voyage	trip	voyager	to travel
rapide	rapid, quick		
à pied	on foot		

Unit 6

Comment allez-vous au travail?

How do you get to work?

1. Listen to these young people telling Sylvie how they get to school, what time they leave home, and how long their trip takes. Match the names with the correct pictures and times.

Because Sylvie is speaking to younger people she uses the **tu** or familiar form.

Marie-Claude   Françoise   Delphine

Tu prends le bus pour aller au collège?	Do you take the bus to school?
Tu quittes la maison à quelle heure?	What time do you leave the house?
Le voyage dure combien de temps?	How long does the trip take?
à peu près	about

2. Sylvie is making some incorrect statements. Use the negative **ne** (verb) **pas** construction to tell her so and give the correct answer.

Example: Laurent prend le métro.
Non, il ne prend pas le métro, il va en vélo.

a. Marie-Claude prend le bus.

b. Françoise quitte la maison à 8 heures.

3. *Now listen to these people saying how they get to work and how long it takes. Notice that the interviewer uses the **vous** form because he is talking to adults. Link up the method of transport with the correct journey time, then practice answering the questions yourself.*

Je peux vous poser une question?
May I ask you a question?

Il vous faut combien de temps?
How long does it take you?

une bonne demi-heure
a good half-hour

trois quarts d'heure
three-quarters of an hour

disons …
let's say …

Ça dépend.
It depends.

dans le coin
in the vicinity

4. *Now it's your turn to conduct a survey. What words are missing from the following questions? Use the correct form of the verb in brackets for (a) interviewing an adult and (b) interviewing a child.*

Pour aller au travail?	Pour aller au collège?
(a) Vous	(b) Tu
Vous _____ le bus? (prendre)	Tu _____ le car de ramassage?
Vous _____ à quelle heure? (partir)	Tu _____ à quelle heure?
Vous _____ à quelle heure? (arriver)	Tu _____ à quelle heure?

Unit 6   **89**

5. *Listen to these people discussing the best way to go to work. What do they say about each method of transport? Complete the sentences.*

a. Je préfère _____ parce que _____.
b. Je préfère _____ parce que _____.
c. Je préfère _____ parce que _____.
d. Je préfère _____ parce que _____.
e. Je préfère _____ parce que _____.
f. Je préfère _____ parce que _____.
g. Je préfère _____ parce que _____.

C'est bon pour la santé.	It's good for your health.
C'est moins cher.	It's less expensive.
C'est plus rapide.	It's faster.
C'est plus pratique.	It's more practical.
C'est plus confortable.	It's more comfortable.
C'est rapide.	It's fast.
Il n'y a pas de problème avec le parking.	There's no problem with parking.

Pronunciation

Rappel! *Remember the final* **d**, **s**, *and* **t** *are not usually sounded.*

Listen and repeat the parts of the verb **partir**.

Now listen and repeat the parts of the verb **prendre**. *Notice how the "e" sound changes in the* **nous** *and* **vous** *forms and in the third person plural (***ils/elles***).*

Now listen and repeat **arriver**. *How many of the forms of* **arriver** *sound the same?*

Close-up

Arriver, to arrive, is a regular **-er** verb

j'arriv<u>e</u>	nous arriv<u>ons</u>
tu arriv<u>es</u>	vous arriv<u>ez</u>
il arriv<u>e</u>	ils arriv<u>ent</u>
elle arriv<u>e</u>	elles arriv<u>ent</u>

Partir, to leave is a regular **-ir** verb

je par<u>s</u>	nous part<u>ons</u>
tu par<u>s</u>	vous part<u>ez</u>
il par<u>t</u>	ils part<u>ent</u>
elle par<u>t</u>	elles part<u>ent</u>

*__Prendre__, to take, is an irregular **-re** verb

Notice how the stem changes in the **nous, vous, ils,** and **elles** forms:

je pr<u>ends</u>	nous pr<u>enons</u>
tu pr<u>ends</u>	vous pr<u>enez</u>
il pr<u>end</u>	ils pr<u>ennent</u>
elle pr<u>end</u>	elles pr<u>ennent</u>

*All verbs ending in **-prendre** will follow this pattern, e.g., **apprendre**, to learn, **comprendre**, to understand, **reprendre**, to resume.

Tu and *vous*

There are two ways of saying "you" in French.

Vouvoyer (to call someone **vous**) is the polite form used for people you don't know very well. You will need this form most.

Tutoyer (to call someone **tu**) is used when talking to children, animals, and intimate friends or people you know very well. It is considered bad manners to use the **tu** form when addressing another adult unless you have been invited to do so.

Y

Y (pronounced "ee") is used to mean "there" when it refers to a place already mentioned. It comes in front of the verb:

Comment vas-tu <u>au collège</u>?	J'<u>y</u> vais en voiture.
Comment allez-vous <u>en ville</u>?	J'<u>y</u> vais en bus.
M. Bernard va <u>au travail</u> à pied?	Oui, il <u>y</u> va à pied.

On prend le bus ou le métro?

Shall we take the bus or the subway?

RECORDING 1. *What is the best way to these places? Listen and find out which subway you need, and when it runs.*

a. La Tour Eiffel

b. L'Arc de Triomphe

c. Les Halles

d. Le Sacré-Cœur

Word Bank

le billet	*ticket*	l'horaire *m.*	*schedule*
le carnet	*"booklet" of tickets*	la ligne	*line*
la correspondance	*connection*	le ticket	*ticket*
la direction	*direction*		

92 French

2.

A vous! *Now you ask which subway you need to go to these places and how long it takes. Write down what you would say first, then listen again to check you have it right.*

Le musée d'Orsay   Le Louvre

La Cité des Sciences   Les Halles

Quelle est la ligne?/C'est quelle ligne?
Which line is it?

Il faut combien de temps?
How long does it take?

Il faut compter …
It could take … (lit: you have to count)

C'est gentil.
That's nice of you.

Merci.
(No) thank you.

Unit 6

3. Listen and find out whether it's the right bus. Match the pictures with the conversation, then write down what information each speaker is given.

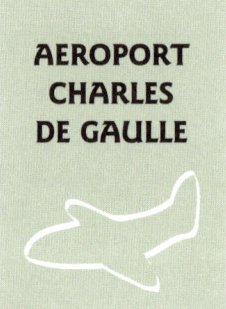
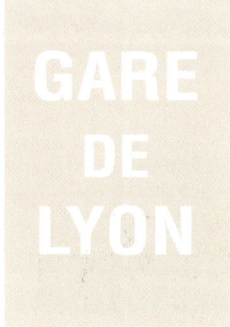

C'est bien le bus pour … ?
Is this the right bus for … ?

Vous avez besoin de …
You need to …

C'est direct?
Is it direct?

Il y a un bus tous les combien?
How often does the bus run?

Ouais.
Yeah.

Il faut changer.
It is necessary to change.

Il vous faut le 5.
You need number 5.

Did You Know?

In Paris you use the same tickets for the bus and subway. It is cheaper to buy a **carnet** ("booklet"), which is a set of ten tickets for the price of seven. There is a map at each bus stop showing the bus route and indicating how many tickets you need for any journey. When you get on the bus you have to validate (**composter**) your ticket by putting it in a machine which stamps the date and time on it. You can also buy a **carte touristique** if you are staying in Paris for two, four, or seven days.

Each of the 15 subway lines is designated by its terminal stations, e.g., Porte de Clignancourt, Porte d'Orléans. To check which direction to follow, look for the name of the last station on the line you need. The **RER (Réseau Express Régional)** is a fast subway network which goes further into the suburbs around Paris. It's more expensive to travel on the RER.

French

4. *Listen carefully to some subway routes being described.*

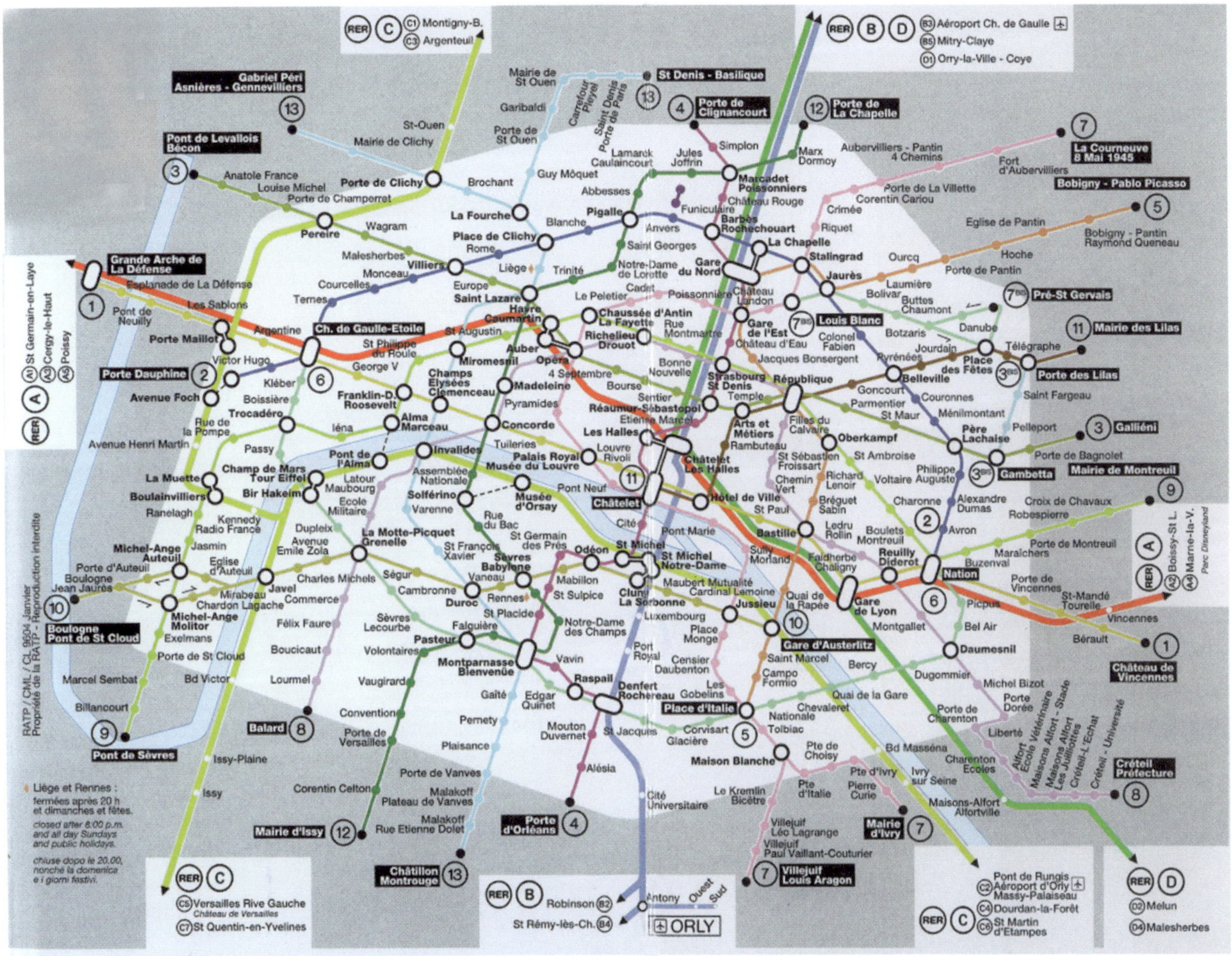

[Paris metro map]

de ... à
from ... to

5. *Listen to the recording for activity 4 again. Here are some answers which need questions. Write down which line you take to arrive at your destination.*

   a. Le Tour Eiffel
   b. L'Arc de Triomphe
   c. Le Sacré-Coeur
   d. Le Louvre

Unit 6   95

Pronunciation

Listen and repeat the names of some of the sights in Paris:

la Tour Eiffel
l'Arc de Triomphe
le Sacré-Cœur
Notre-Dame

le Louvre
le musée d'Orsay
la Cité des Sciences
les Halles

Now listen and repeat some of the names of subway stations:

Château de Vincennes
Porte d'Orléans

Pont de Neuilly
Porte de Clignancourt

Close-up

To say you need something:

avoir besoin de, *to have need of*

J'<u>ai besoin d'</u>un plan de la ville. I need a town map.

You can also use the construction **Il** *(vous)* **faut** *... , it is necessary (for you) ...*

<u>Il</u> vous <u>faut</u> un horaire. You need a schedule.

Rappel! *Before masculine nouns* **à** *changes to* **au**:

à + le Louvre = <u>au</u> Louvre

Before nouns beginning with a vowel or "h" **à** *becomes* **à l'**:

à + l'Arc de Triomphe = <u>à l'</u>Arc de Triomphe

Before plural nouns **à** *becomes* **aux**:

à + les Halles = <u>aux</u> Halles

Rappel! *The word for "there" referring to a place already mentioned is* **y**. *It goes in front of the verb:*

Il faut combien de temps pour <u>y</u> aller? How long does it take to go there?

In conversation **on** *(one/we) is often used instead of* **nous** *(we). It is followed by the third person singular (***il/elle*** form) of the verb:*

We are going to Paris. Nous allons à Paris.
       OR <u>On va</u> à Paris.

Prendre un taxi ou louer une voiture?

Take a taxi or rent a car?

Word Bank

le car	long-distance bus	quand?	when?
la circulation	traffic	aider	to help
le permis de conduire	driver's license	s'appeler	to be called
la pièce d'identité	identity card	*vouloir	to want
la représentation	performance (of a play)	partir	to leave
le théâtre	theater	louer	to rent
les travaux	roadworks	conduire	to drive
le vol	flight		

1. *Listen to these people at the hotel reception asking to book taxis. Where do they want to go? Put the right number under each picture.*

_____   _____   _____   _____

Le vol part à …	The flight leaves at …
La représentation commence à …	The perfomance begins at …
C'est loin?	Is it far?
Il pleut.	It's raining.
à cause des travaux	because of the roadworks
beaucoup de circulation	a lot of traffic
à cette heure-ci	at this time
une heure d'avance	one hour ahead

2. Listen again and find out how long each journey is going to take and what the problem is. Match the stop watches with the correct picture.

3. **A vous!** *Here is the number of the local taxi firm. Call and book a taxi. Prepare what you would say first, then practice saying it aloud.*

> *Radio Taxis 01 12 34 56 78*
>
> *You want a taxi to go to the airport.*
>
> *Your flight leaves at 17:45.*
>
> *You want to know how long it will take.*
>
> *You want to know how much it will cost.*

4. *You've decided to rent a car to go to Chartres for the day. Listen to Sylvie making the arrangements. What does the rental agent want to know? Put these questions in the right order.*

Vous voulez la voiture pour combien de jours?
For how many days do you want the car?

Vous la voulez quand exactement?
When do you want it exactly?

Quelle sorte de voiture voulez-vous?
What sort of car do you want?

Comment vous appelez-vous?
What is your name?

Votre adresse?
Your address?

Pour combien de personnes?
For how many people?

Comment voulez-vous payer?
How do you want to pay?

Vous avez votre permis de conduire avec vous?
Do you have your driver's license with you?

5. *Listen again and put Sylvie's answers in the right order.*

Sylvie Verlaine.

Hôtel du Parc, rue St-Denis.

Avec une carte de crédit.

De vendredi à lundi.

Trois jours.

Une grande voiture.

Oui, je l'ai ici.

Six personnes.

6. **A vous!** *Now it's your turn to rent a car. This is what you want. Prepare your answers and then practice them saying them aloud.*

Pronunciation

Listen to Sylvie saying the parts of the verb **vouloir.** *Which parts of the verb sound the same? Which parts do you think will be the most useful to remember?*

Now practice saying the question words after Sylvie.

Close-up

***vouloir**—to want

je v<u>eux</u>	nous v<u>oulons</u>
tu v<u>eux</u>	vous v<u>oulez</u>
il v<u>eut</u>	ils v<u>eulent</u>
elle v<u>eut</u>	elles v<u>eulent</u>

Voulez-vous ... ?	*Do you want to ... ?*
Que voulez-vous?	*What do you want?*
Je voudrais ...	*I would like ...*

Rappel! *Remember that* **on** *can be used in conversation to mean "we":*

<u>On</u> veut ...	*We want ...*

Question words

<u>Combien</u>?	*How much/how many?*
C'est <u>combien</u>?	*How much is it?*
<u>Quel/Quelle</u> ... ?	*What ... ?*
<u>Quel</u> est votre nom?	*What is your name?*
<u>Quelle</u> sorte de voiture?	*What kind of car?*
<u>Quand</u>	*When?*
<u>Quand</u> voulez-vous partir?	*When do you want to leave?*
<u>Que</u> ... ?	*What ... ?*
<u>Que</u> voulez-vous?	*What do you want?*
<u>Comment</u>?	*How?*
<u>Comment</u> voulez-vous payer?	*How do you want to pay?*
<u>Où</u>	*Where?*

Checkpoints

Use the check list to test what you've learned in this unit and review anything you're not sure of.

Can you ... ? Yes No

- *say how you travel to work/school* .... ❏ ...... ❏
  Je pars à ...
  J'y vais à pied.
  en voiture
  Je prends le train.
  Je prends le métro.
  Je prends le bus.
  J'arrive à ...

- *say how you prefer to travel* .... ❏ ...... ❏
  Je préfère aller ...

- *and why* .... ❏ ...... ❏
  parce que ...

- *it's faster/cheaper* .... ❏ ...... ❏
  C'est plus rapide/moins cher.

- *ask which (subway or bus) line to take ...* .... ❏ ...... ❏
  C'est quelle ligne pour aller à ... ?

- *ask how long it takes* .... ❏ ...... ❏
  Il faut combien de temps?

- *ask how much it costs* .... ❏ ...... ❏
  Ça coûte combien?

- *ask if this is the right bus* .... ❏ ...... ❏
  C'est bien le bus pour ... ?

- *ask if it is direct* .... ❏ ...... ❏
  C'est direct?

- *and how often it runs* .... ❏ ...... ❏
  Il y a un bus tous les combien?

- *tell someone which subway to take* .... ❏ ...... ❏
  Vous prenez la direction ...

- *and where you get off* .... ❏ ...... ❏
  et descendez à ...

- *and where they have to change* .... ❏ ...... ❏
  Il faut changer à ...

French

Can you ... ?   Yes   No

- ask how often it runs .... ☐ ...... ☐
  Toutes les dix minutes.

- say when your flight leaves .... ☐ ...... ☐
  Le vol part à …

- ask where someone wants to go .... ☐ ...... ☐
  Où voulez-vous aller?

- ask if it is far .... ☐ ...... ☐
  C'est loin?

Learning tips

When you listen to people speaking your own language you don't always listen carefully to every word they say. You listen only to the key words you need to hear and your brain "fills in" the rest. When learning a new language your brain doesn't have enough information to fill in for you and you have to listen more carefully. In fact, you have to learn to listen all over again, which can be very tiring. Don't do too much at one time.

As the listening texts are getting longer and spoken at more normal speed, you cannot expect to be able to distinguish every word. Most people do not speak clearly all the time, so don't be discouraged if you don't catch every word first time! Listen first for the key words, then listen again and again until you can fill in most of the other words and get the "gist" of what is being said.

Do you want to learn more?

Look through any French-language newspapers and magazines you have for advertisements, listings for theaters, restaurants, travel agents, etc. Think through what you would say if you were calling to make a reservation.

For more practice, see Extra! on page A12.

1 Extra!

le nord	north
le sud	south
l'est	east
l'ouest	west
dans le centre	in the middle
dans l'est	in the east
à côté de	next to, beside
près de	near

> Il y a plus de 200 millions de francophones dans le monde.
>
> Le français arrive en neuvième position des langues parlées après le chinois, l'anglais, le hindi, l'espagnol, le russe, l'arabe, le portugais et le japonais.

francophone	a French speaker
le monde	the world
neuvième	ninth

1. Listen to the recording. Then match the names to the places on the map.

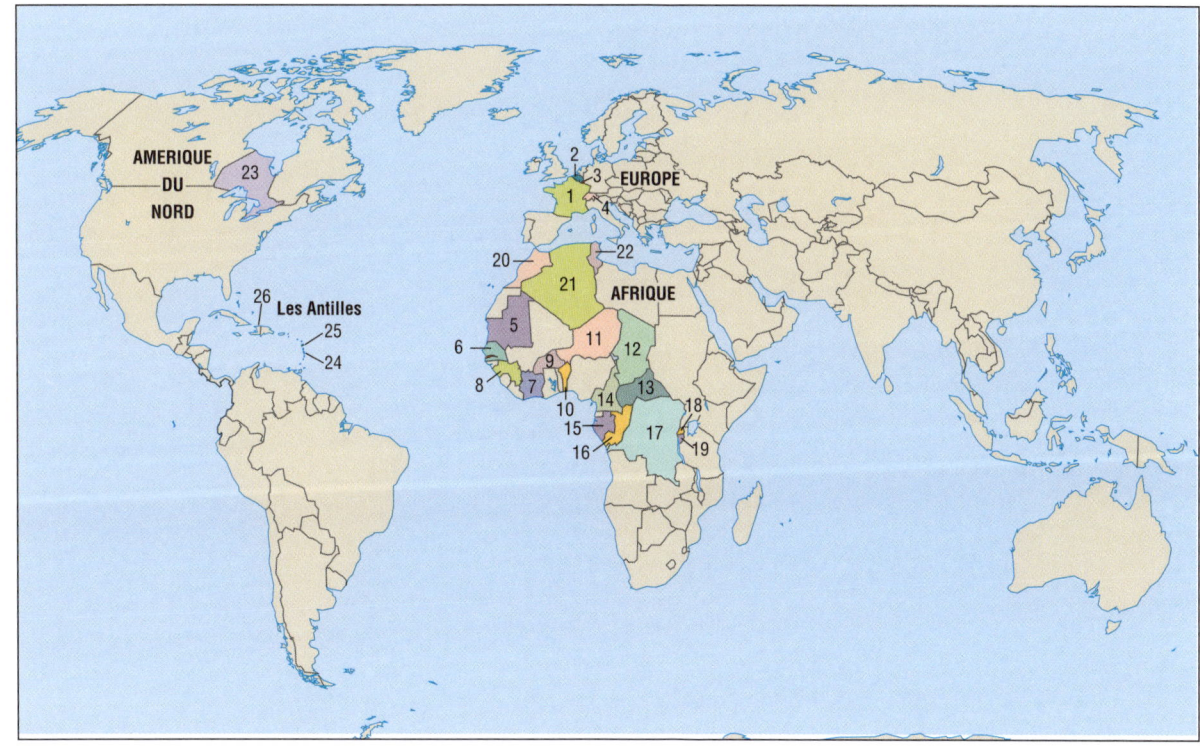

En Europe:
la France
la Belgique
le Luxembourg
la Suisse

En Amérique du Nord:
le Québec

Aux Antilles:
la Martinique
la Guadeloupe
St.-Martin
Haïti

En Afrique:
la Mauritanie
le Sénégal
la Côte d'Ivoire
la Guinée
le Burkina Faso
le Bénin
le Niger
le Tchad
la République Centrafricaine
le Cameroun
le Gabon
le Congo
la République Démocratique du Congo
le Rwanda
le Burundi
la Tunisie
l'Algérie
le Maroc

RECORDING 2. *Listen to the recording. Beside each place put:*

M for **langue maternelle**—*native language*

O for **langue officielle**—*official language*

A for **langue administrative**—*language used in administration*

pour cent	percent
ou … ou	either … or
comme	as

3. *Listen to the presenter introducing the contestants for a quiz show. Where are they from?*

Jean-Marc   Noura   Catherine

Benoît   Virginie   Nadjet

les concurrents	*contestants*
pour	*for*
les étudiants	*students*
Qui le sait?	*Who knows?*
les représentants	*representatives*
Je ne peux pas accepter ça.	*I can't accept that.*
dans l'océan Indien	*in the Indian Ocean*

Extra!

2 Extra!

RECORDING 1. These bottles of wine are out of order. Listen to the recording and put them in the correct order. Listen to find out which wine is in which bottle.

C'est quel vin?	Which wine is it?
premier/première	first
dernier/dernière	last

RECORDING 2. How much does each bottle of wine cost?

a. Nuits St Georges
b. Château Margaux
c. Médoc
d. Beaujolais Villages
e. Chablis 1er cru
f. Pommard 1er cru
g. Sauternes
h. Mouton Cadet
i. Mouton Cadet grand cru

cher/pas cher	*expensive/cheap*
quelque chose de pas cher	*something inexpensive*
Ça, c'est autre chose.	*That's something else (altogether).*

3. **Savoir déguster le vin ...** *Know how to taste wine.*

a. L'œil. Regarder le vin. On boit le vin dans un verre blanc.

b. On tourne. On tourne le verre pour oxygéner le vin pour qu'il exhale son bouquet.

c. Le nez. Plongez le nez dans le verre et respirez.

d. Le goût. Prenez une bonne gorgée et appréciez sa texture et sa saveur.

e. Cracher. Si vous voulez déguster plusieurs vins sérieusement, il faut cracher.

f. Et surtout ne fumez pas. Les cigarettes gâchent votre goût.

boire	*to drink*
cracher	*to spit*
déguster	*to taste*
exhaler	*to emit*
fumer	*to smoke*
gâcher	*to spoil*
oxygéner	*to oxygenate*
plonger	*to plunge*
regarder	*to look at*
respirer	*to breathe*
sentir	*to taste*
tourner	*to turn*
le bouquet	*bouquet, aroma*
il faut …	*it is necessary to …*
la gorgée	*mouthful*
le goût	*sense of taste*
le nez	*nose*
l'œil	*eye*
plusieurs	*several*
la saveur	*flavor*
surtout	*above all*

3 Extra!

le cirque	*circus*
la croisière	*cruise*
la fleur	*flower*
le hockey sur glace	*ice hockey*
les installations olympiques	*the Olympic installations*
le jardin botanique	*botanical garden*
le manège	*merry-go-round*
le match de foot	*soccer game*
le parc d'attractions	*amusement park*
la patinoire	*ice rink*
la visite guidée	*guided tour*
la vue	*view*
le vieux port	*the old port*
en été	*in summer*
peut-être	*perhaps*
magnifique	*magnificent*
ouvert	*open*
adorer	*to adore*
avoir l'intention de	*to intend to*
faire du patin à glace	*to go ice-skating*
jouer au tennis	*to play tennis*

1. These people are talking about what they could do in Montréal. Listen to their conversation and number the activities in the order in which they are suggested.

On pourrait visiter le parc olympique.

On pourrait visiter le parc d'attractions La Ronde.

On pourrait faire une visite du vieux port ou bien une croisière sur le Saint-Laurent.

Qu'est-ce qu'il y a à voir?   What is there to see?

Did You Know?

The island of Montréal, situated on the St. Lawrence River in Canada, is dominated by a hill which was called the Mount Royal (Mont réal), from which it gets its name. Note that the "t" is not pronounced at the end of the word Mont.

Extra! **A7**

2. *What is everyone going to do? Listen and find out.*

3. *What could they do this evening? Listen and find out.*

4. *What are these people going to do this evening? Listen and find out.*

5. *Listen to the recording for activity 4 again and find out who each person is going to go out with.*

6. *You are spending a weekend in Montréal. What would you like to do? With whom would you like to go? Complete the following sentence and practice saying it aloud.*

Je voudrais _____ avec _____.

4 Extra!

1. Some visitors to Guadeloupe are in the tourist information office asking about places to visit. Listen to the information they are given and write down the suggested places they should visit.

Il vaut mieux louer une voiture.   *It's better to rent a car.*

5 Extra!

1. *These models are going on a photo shoot. Who is taking what?*

le bikini	*bikini*
le jean	*denim jeans*
le maillot	*swimsuit*
le motif	*pattern*
le short	*shorts*
à rayures	*striped*
découpé(e)	*cut-off*
vieux/vieille	*old*
également	*also, as well*
Personne ne veut …	*Nobody wants …*

2. Who are these people? Listen to the descriptions and pick out who's who from the illustration.

Mme Boussard
Mme Crance
M. Dupont
M. Maillard
Mlle Meugeot
M. Proudhon

Qui est-ce?	Who is it?
Il est assez grand, lui aussi.	He is also quite tall.
le porte-documents	briefcase
le téléphone portatif	mobile phone
l'homme aux cheveux bruns	the man with brown hair
le costume	man's suit
l'ensemble *m.*	outfit
gris foncé	dark gray
les chaussures à hauts talons/à talons bas	high-heeled shoes/flat shoes
Il tient un journal à la main.	He is holding a newspaper in his hand.

Extra!

6 Extra!

1. *Listen to Jean-Claude telling you about his trip to work and cross out the phrases that don't apply.*

   a. Le voyage dure (dix minutes/un quart d'heure/une demi-heure/trois quarts d'heure).

   b. J'y vais (en voiture/en métro/en vélo/en bus).

   c. Je pars à (sept heures/sept heures et quart/sept heures vingt/sept heures et demie) et je vais (à l'arrêt de bus/à la station de métro/au garage/sortir mon vélo).

   d. Je prends (le bus/le métro) direction Château de Vincennes, qui passe toutes les (cinq/dix/quinze/vingt) minutes.

   e. J'arrive à huit heures (moins dix/moins le quart/moins vingt/moins cinq).

   le trajet journalier   *the daily trip*

2. **A vous!** *Listen again to what Jean-Claude says and then adapt the text to describe a regular trip you make. Don't forget to practice reading your text aloud.*

3. *Listen to this television presenter summing up a studio discussion. For each person, write down where they live (if mentioned) and how they get to work.*

4. *Now you make a report about where your friends live and how they get to work. Practice reading it aloud.*

Test 1:
Review of Units 1–3

1. **Comment ça va?** *How would you say how you are?*

1.  2.  3.

- *a.* Pas mal.
- *b.* Très bien merci.
- *c.* Ça ne va pas.

2. **C'est quelle question?** *Match the question and answer.*

1. Comment vous appelez-vous?
2. Vous habitez où?
3. Vous êtes français?
4. Parlez-vous anglais?

- *a.* J'habite aux Etats-Unis.
- *b.* Oui, un peu.
- *c.* Je m'appelle Wenders.
- *d.* Non, je suis hollandais.

3. *Put the days of the week into the right order.*

- *a.* mardi
- *b.* dimanche
- *c.* mercredi
- *d.* jeudi
- *e.* samedi
- *f.* lundi
- *g.* vendredi

4. **Je voudrais ...** *What would you ask for?*

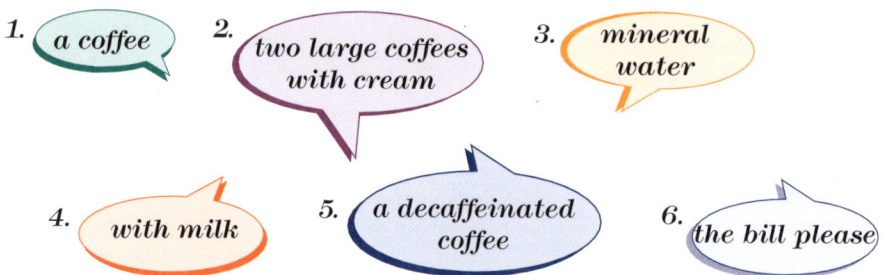

a. un déca

b. avec du lait

c. l'addition s'il vous plaît

d. deux grands crèmes

e. un café

f. de l'eau minérale

5. **Le**, **la**, *or* **l'**?

1. un hôtel—_____ hôtel
2. un jus d'orange—_____ jus d'orange
3. une bière—_____ bière
4. un sandwich au jambon—_____ sandwich
5. une omelette au fromage—_____ omelette
6. une tarte aux pommes—_____ tarte
7. un verre de vin rouge—_____ verre
8. une bouteille de vin blanc—_____ bouteille

6. **Au**, **à la**, *or* **aux**?

1. une omelette _____ jambon
2. une tarte _____ pommes
3. une glace _____ vanille
4. un sandwich _____ fromage

7.

Je suis ... *What should they say?*

1. I am a policeman.
2. I am unemployed.
3. I work in education.
4. I am a sales assistant.
5. I am self-employed.
6. I work in information technology.
7. I work in a hospital.

a. Je suis informaticien(ne).
b. Je suis agent de police.
c. Je suis vendeur/se.
d. Je suis au chômage.
e. Je travaille à mon compte.
f. Je travaille dans un hôpital.
g. Je travaille dans l'enseignement.

8.

Travailler—*to work. A regular -er verb. Can you add the right endings?*

Je travaill_____   nous travaill_____

tu travaill_____   vous travaill_____

il/elle travaill_____   ils/elles travaill_____

9.

What are the feminine equivalents of these words?

1. le mari
2. le frère
3. le père
4. le fils
5. l'infirmier
6. le boulanger
7. l'électricien
8. le coiffeur

10. Mon, ma, *or* mes?

1. _____ frère
2. _____ femme
3. _____ ami
4. _____ enfants
5. _____ amie
6. _____ chien
7. _____ sœur

11. *Saying "no." Make these statements negative.*

1. Oui, je suis marié(e).
2. Il habite à Paris.
3. Je sais!
4. Je travaille à mon compte.
5. Je veux aller au cinéma.
6. Elle est comptable.

Test 2:
Review of Units 4–6

1. *Vocabulary. Pair up these words.*

l'arrêt d'autobus	*gas station*
l'église *(f)*	*town*
la gare	*bus stop*
la pharmacie	*train station*
la station service	*pharmacy*
la ville	*church*

2. *Where? Choose the right answers.*

1. Pour aller à la gare?
2. La piscine est près d'ici?
3. Il y a une poste près d'ici?
4. Pour une pharmacie?
5. Est-ce qu'il y a un cinéma?

a. Ah non, il faut prendre le bus.
b. Il faut aller en ville.
c. En face de l'hôtel.
d. Il n'y a pas de gare ici.
e. Tout près, à gauche.

3. **Pour aller à … ?** *Fill in the correct form:* **à la**, **au**, *or* **à l'**.

1. _____ gare
2. _____ aéroport
3. _____ plage
4. _____ parking
5. _____ syndicat d'initiative
6. _____ hôtel

4. **Trouvez la bonne direction.** *Find the right directions.*

1.   2.   3.

4.   5.

   a. Vous allez tout droit

   b. Vous traversez le pont

   c. Vous tournez à droite

   d. Vous prenez la première rue à droite

   e. Vous tournez à gauche

5. **J'ai oublié …** *What have you forgotten? Fill in the right form:* **mon**, **ma**, *or* **mes**.

1. _____ après-shampooing

2. _____ lunettes de soleil

3. _____ brosse à dents

4. _____ dentifrice

5. _____ kleenex

6. _____ sèche-cheveux

6. **Je voudrais …** *I would like … Fill in the correct form:* **blanc**, **blanche**, **blancs**, *or* **blanches**.

1. une chemise _____

2. des chaussettes _____

3. un pull _____

4. une veste _____

5. des gants _____

7. *What were the questions? Complete the dialog.*

1. Bonjour. Je voudrais un pull.
2. Quarante-deux.
3. En noir.
4. Oui, c'est tout.

a. Quelle taille?
b. Quelle couleur?
c. Que désirez-vous?
d. C'est tout?

8. **Il** *or* **elle**, **ils**, *or* **elles**? *Put in the right form.*

1. Le pull: _____ est trop long.
2. La veste: _____ est trop courte.
3. Le pantalon: _____ est trop cher.
4. Les chemises: _____ sont en soie.
5. Les sandwichs: _____ sont délicieux.
6. Monsieur Dubois: _____ est grand.

9. **Tu** *or* **vous**? *Put in the right form.*

1. _____ prenez le bus?
2. _____ arrives à quelle heure?
3. _____ prends le car de ramassage?
4. _____ allez en ville?
5. _____ pars à quelle heure?
6. _____ vas au cinéma?

10. *Complete the dialog by adding the right question.*

1. Le Louvre? Il faut prendre le bus.
2. Ligne 14.
3. Non, il faut changer à la place de la République.
4. Non, le bus pour l'Opéra est là-bas.
5. Toutes les dix minutes.
6. Un plan. Oui, le voilà.

a. Avez-vous un plan de la ville?
b. C'est bien le bus pour l'Opéra?
c. C'est direct?
d. C'est quelle ligne?
e. Il y a un bus tous les combien?
f. Pour aller au Louvre?

11. *Question words. Fill in the right question word.*

1. _____ sorte de voiture voulez-vous?
2. Pour _____ de personnes?
3. _____ voulez-vous partir?
4. _____ voulez-vous?
5. _____ voulez-vous payer?
6. _____ habitez-vous?

Answer Key

Unit 1

Pages 2–4

1. 1. early evening/just met; 2. the daytime/just met; 3. later at night/saying goodnight and leaving; 4. two friends greeting/any time of day

2. a. 2; b. 3; c. 4; d. 1; e. 5

3. a. 4; b. 3; c. 2; d. 1

4. 1. x; 2.—; 3.—; 4. ✓

6. Bonjour; Ça va *or* Pas mal *or* Comme ci comme ça; monsieur

    Bonsoir; très bien; mademoiselle

    Bonsoir; madame; Ah, non, ça ne va pas; bonne nuit madame

Pages 7–9

1. a. Gilles Bernard, la Suisse; b. Sylvie Verlaine, la France; c. Lucienne Briand, La Belgique; d. Patrice Millerioux, le Canada

2. Je vous présente M. Gilles Bernard, il est <u>suisse</u> et il habite à <u>Genève</u> en <u>Suisse</u>.

    Voici Mme Briand. Elle est <u>belge</u> et elle habite <u>à Bruxelles en Belgique</u>.

    Voici Mlle Verlaine. Elle est <u>française</u> et habite <u>à Paris en France</u>.

    Voici M. Millerioux. Il est <u>canadien</u> et habite <u>à Québec au Canada</u>.

3. Non, il n'est pas américain. Il est suisse.

    Non, elle n'est pas suisse. Elle est belge.

    Non, il n'est pas anglais. Il est canadien.

4. a. Bonjour. Je m'appelle Gérard et je suis <u>français</u>. J'habite à Rouen et je parle français et <u>anglais</u>.

    b. Moi? Je <u>m'appelle</u> Anja et je <u>suis</u> allemande. J'<u>habite</u> à Berlin <u>en</u> Allemagne. Je parle allemand et un peu de <u>français</u>.

    c. J'<u>habite</u> à New York aux Etats-Unis. Je m'appelle Nigel <u>et</u> Je suis <u>américain</u>. Je ne <u>parle</u> pas français.

    d. Je m'appelle Kenji et j'habite à Tokyo <u>au</u> Japon. Je <u>suis</u> japonais et je parle japonais et <u>anglais</u>.

    e. Moi? Je m'appelle <u>Rosa</u>. Non, je ne suis pas espagnole. Je suis brésilienne. J'habite à <u>Rio</u> au <u>Brésil</u>. Je parle portugais, anglais et <u>un peu</u> de français.

5. Vous habitez … ? Parlez-vous (français/anglais/japonais)?

    Vous êtes … ? Comment vous appelez-vous?

Pages 13–14

1. 1. Graham; 2. Schwartz; 3. Fernandez; 4. Rossellini; 5. Macintosh

5. a. Fernandez, 19; b. Macintosh, 13; c. Schwartz, 7; d. Rossellini, 11; e. Graham, 9

Unit 2

Pages 20–22

1. M. Albert—a coffee; Mme Albert—a large light coffee; Nathalie—an orange juice; Delphine—a hot chocolate; M. Albert—four croissants

2. 1. two large light coffees; 2. a coffee, a hot chocolate, and 2 croissants; 3. a beer and a carbonated mineral water; 4. an orange juice and a croissant; 5. a decaffeinated coffee, a light coffee, a tea with milk, and two croissants; 6. 4 coffees

3. Je voudrais un grand crème.

    Deux express, s'il vous plaît.

    Un thé au lait, s'il vous plaît.

    Deux cafés.

    Avez-vous des croissants?

    Je voudrais un déca.

    Une bière, s'il vous plaît.

    Un Coca et de l'eau minérale gazeuse.

4. vingt-quatre; trente-six; vingt-huit; quarante-sept; trente-neuf; vingt et un

5. L'addition, s'il vous plaît!; €9,20

6. Avez-vous de l'eau minérale; gazeuse, s'il vous plaît; Je voudrais un crème; grand

Pages 25–27

1. jambon, fromage, saucisson.
   a ham sandwich, a cheese sandwich, a draught beer, a red wine

2. Qu'est-ce que vous avez comme sandwichs/salades/glaces?

4. 1. a salad niçoise and a sparkling mineral water
   2. a steak and fries and a pitcher of red wine
   3. two hamburgers, a serving of fries, a cola, a vanilla milk-shake.
   4. an omelet with mixed herbs, a seafood salad, tea with lemon, a draught beer

5. 1. a strawberry ice cream; 2. nothing; 3. 2 apple pies; 4. a lemon pie and a chocolate ice cream with whipped cream

7. Table 1—c. €13,50; Table 2—a. €7; Table 3—e. €14,50; Table 4—b. €11,60; Table 5—d. €13,70

Pages 29–32

1. She buys Le Figaro and Télépoche and asks for the New York Herald but the news agent doesn't have one.

2. Le Télérama, €1,60; Paris Match, €3; Marie-Claire, €3; Le Figaro, €1,20

3. a. €1,40; b. €1,50; c. €1,20; d. €1

4. Gilles—a town map, €1,50, a packet of sweets and an orangina, €7,45
   Sylvie—5 post cards and 5 stamps

5. Avez-vous un plan de Paris? Avez-vous des télécartes? Avez-vous le New York Herald? Je voudrais trois cartes postales et trois timbres pour les États-Unis. Je voudrais du chocolat. Un coca.

6. Coca-cola, €2,50; Orangina €2,50; post cards, 80 cents; telephone cards, €7,40 or €14,75; a town map, €1,50; newspaper €1,20; sweets (Carambar) €3,45

Unit 3

Pages 38–41

1. a. agent de police; b. coiffeuse; c. homme d'affaires; d. médecin; e. étudiant

2. Gilles Bernard—employé de banque, une banque
   Sylvie Verlaine—infirmière, un hôpital
   Lucienne Briand—dessinatrice de BD, un atelier
   Patrice Millerioux—directeur des ressources humaines, une entreprise

3. a. Carmen Fernandez—Je suis informaticienne et je travaille dans une entreprise.
   b. Paul Black—Je suis guide touristique et je travaille dans un bureau de tourisme.
   c. Mme Rossi—Je suis vendeuse et je travaille dans un grand magasin.
   d. Jack Nicholls—Je suis agent de police et je travaille dans un commissariat de police.

5. a. M. Bernard, de Genève en Suisse. Il est <u>employé de banque</u> et travaille dans <u>une banque</u>.
   b. Mme Rossi, de Rome en Italie. Elle est <u>vendeuse</u> et travaille dans <u>un grand magasin</u>.
   c. M. Nicholls, de New York. Il est <u>agent de police</u> et travaille <u>dans un commissariat de police</u>.
   d. Mlle Verlaine, de Paris. Elle est <u>infirmière</u> et travaille dans <u>un hôpital</u>.
   e. Mlle Briand, de Bruxelles en Belgique. Elle est <u>dessinatrice</u> et travaille dans <u>un atelier</u>.
   f. Mlle Fernandez, de Madrid en Espagne. Elle est <u>informaticienne</u> et travaille dans <u>un bureau</u>.
   g. M. Millerioux, de Québec au Canada. Il est <u>directeur des ressources humaines</u> et travaille dans <u>une grande entreprise</u>.
   h. M. Black, de Londres en Angleterre. Il est <u>guide touristique</u> et travaille dans un <u>bureau de tourisme</u>.

6. le secteur automobile—le/la mécanicien(ne)
   la bureautique—le/la secrétaire
   le commerce—le/la comptable
   le droit—l'avocat
   l'enseignement—le professeur
   l'hôtellerie—le/la cuisinier(ère)
   l'informatique—l'informaticien(ne)
   les médias—le/la journaliste
   les postes et télécommunications—l'agent des postes
   la santé—l'infirmier(ère)
   les sciences et techniques—le/la scientifique

Pages 43–46

1. a. Gilles—32, divorced; b. Isabella—35, married, 6-year-old son; c. Paul—28, single; d. Jack—36, separated; e. Lucienne—33, married, two children; f. Carmen—28, single; g. Patrice—32, two children, married; h. Sylvie—24, single

3. On the right is his son Didier; beside him is his father, Jean-Claude; beside his father is his mother, Murielle; and between Didier and his wife, Véronique, is his daughter Elodie; on the left is their dog, Samuel, or Sam for short.

4. Didier, 4; Murielle, 51; Jean-Claude, 55; Elodie, 2; Véronique, 30; Patrice, 32

5. Pictures a and c were Thierry's; b and d were Sylvie's.

6. ma; *name*; *age*; mon; *name*; *age*; *open answer*

Pages 48–51

1. they could go—to a restaurant; dancing in a night club; to the movies; for a walk along the Champs-Elysées

2. a. Gilles Bernard—va aller danser; b. Mme Fourrier—va aller au restaurant; c. M. Delafin—va faire une promenade en ville; d. Sylvie Verlaine—va aller en boîte de nuit; e. Mme Coulot—va aller au lit; f. M. Garnier—va aller au cinéma; g. Patrice Millerioux—va rester au bar et boire une bière

3. Answers as in Activity 2.

4. Non, il ne va pas aller au cinéma. Il va rester au bar boire une bière. Non, elle ne va pas visiter la ville. Elle va manger au restaurant. M. Delafin va faire une promenade en ville. Non, Sylvie ne va pas aller à la piscine. Elle va aller en boîte de nuit. Mme Coulot va aller au lit. Non, il ne va pas aller au restaurant. Il va aller au cinéma. Ah, non, il ne va pas aller au cinéma. Il va aller en boîte de nuit avec Sylvie.

Unit 4

Pages 56–58

1. post office ✓; railway station +; pharmacy +; parking ✓; cinema +; bank +

2. 1. a; 2. c; 3. f; 4. b; 5. d; 6. e

3. The bank is beside the cinema.

The gas station is on Napoleon Bonaparte Street in front of the supermarket.

The pharmacy is on Street of the Revolution, opposite the post office.

There is a taxi station on the Avenue Charles de Gaulle in front of the church.

The metro station is on the corner of the rue NB and the Avenue des Chênes.

4. a. La banque est à côté du cinéma.
b. La station service est dans la rue Napoléon Bonaparte devant le supermarché.
c. La pharmacie est dans la rue de la Révolution en face de la poste.
d. La station de taxi est dans l'avenue Charles-de-Gaulle, devant l'église.
e. La station de métro est au coin de la rue N. Bonaparte et de l'avenue des Chênes.

5. a. Il y a une gare près d'ici?
b. Est-ce que la piscine est près d'ici?
c. La poste est près d'ici?
d. Est-ce qu'il y a une pharmacie près d'ici?
e. Il y a un cinéma près d'ici?

Pages 60–62

1. airport; museum; beach; tourist information office; highway; Hotel Mercure

2. a. Pour aller au syndicat d'initiative?; b. Pour aller à l'hôtel Mercure?; c. Pour aller à la plage?; d. Pour aller au musée?; e. Pour aller à l'aéroport?

3. a. 5; b. 1; c. 6; d. 2; e. 4; f. 3

4. a. Vous allez tout droit jusqu'au rond-point et puis vous prenez la première rue à droite.
b. Vous allez tout droit et puis tournez à droite.
c. Vous allez tout droit jusqu'au pont mais vous ne traversez pas le pont. Vous tournez à droite juste avant le pont.
d. Vous prenez la deuxième rue à droite.
e. Vous allez tout droit jusqu'au feu et puis tournez à gauche et traversez le pont.
f. Vous prenez la première rue à gauche et puis tournez à droite.

5. a. à la banque; b. à l'aéroport; c. à la poste; d. à l'hôpital; e. au syndicat d'initiative; f. au musée; g. à l'hôtel; h. à la plage

6. à la tour Eiffel; au musée d'Art moderne; à la gare de Lyon; à la Seine; aux Champs Elysées; au Louvre; à la cathédrale Notre-Dame; au Sacré-Cœur; à l'Arc de Triomphe; au jardin des Tuileries

Pages 64–66

1. Swimming pool—open every day except Monday morning and Thursday evening

   Post office—closed Saturday afternoon and Sunday

   Bakery—closed Sunday afternoon and all day Monday

   Museum—open every day except Thursday and Monday morning

2. la boulangerie 7.00–18.30; la piscine 7.30–21.30; le musée 10.15–17.45; la poste 9.00–18.00

3. le Coq d'Or 18.00–minuit; Le fast-food, 7.00–23.00; La brasserie, 8.00; le restaurant 11.00–22.00

4. Wednesday's Child, 17.30 et 21.50; Happy Days, 19.40 et 23.55; Raging Bull, 17.45 et 21.55; Into the Galaxy; 19.50 et 12.00

5. aujourd'hui: 10.30, 11.45, ou 14.10; demain: 9.30, 12.00, 13.20, 14.40, ou 16.30

6. Le Musée des Beaux-Arts est ouvert tous les jours sauf le mardi. Du lundi au vendredi il ouvre à 10h et ferme à 18h, et samedi et dimanche il ouvre à 10h et il ferme à 16h.

Unit 5

Pages 72–73

1. tissues; hair dryer; toiletry bag, shampoo, conditioner, a hairbrush, a toothbrush, toothpaste, deodorant; toothpaste and deodorant; toiletry bag, razor, aftershave, soap, toothbrush, toothpaste, and a comb.

2. un paquet de mouchoirs en papier €2,80; sèche-cheveux €15,60 and €25,40 (for large); shampooing €2,50; après-shampooing €2,50; brosse €3; brosse à dents €2,80; dentifrice €4,20; rasoir 80 cents; lotion après-rasage €3,50; savon €1; peigne €4,20

3. j'ai oublié mon déodorant/ mon shampooing/mon après-shampooing/ mon dentifrice/mes kleenex.

4. du; en bille/en spray; du; pour les cheveux fins/normaux; oui/merci; du; kleenex/mouchoirs en papier; un paquet/ une boîte

5. déodorant, shampooing, après-shampooing, dentifrice, mouchoirs en papier

Pages 75–76

1. a pair of black pants; a red sweater; white shirt; black dress; dark blue sweatshirt

2. size 42; medium; size 46; size 38; large

3. b. blue sweater, it's cool; a. black pants, they're stylish; b. navy t-shirt, I like the color; a. pink and white striped shirt, it's stylish; a. white t-shirt, it's trendy!

Pages 79–82

1. 1. credit card; 2. traveler's check; 3. cash

2. silk tie, €19,75; striped cotton tie, €15; tartan wool tie, €17,75; brown leather tie, €18

3. red silk scarf, €29,75; wool scarf, €14,50; leather gloves, €24; wool gloves, €13,75; cotton blouse, €29; silk blouse, €39,75

4. a. L'écharpe en <u>soie</u> est <u>plus chère</u> que l'écharpe en laine; b. La chemise en <u>coton</u> est <u>moins chère</u> que la chemise en soie; c. Les gants en <u>cuir</u> sont <u>plus chers</u> que les gants en laine; d. La cravate en <u>cuir marron</u> est <u>moins chère</u> que la cravate en soie rose; e. Le pull en <u>laine</u> est <u>plus cher</u> que le pull en coton.

5. La jupe est trop courte.; Le pull est trop long.; Le pantalon est trop large.; Le jean est trop cher.

6. a. Vous voulez payer comment? Avec un chèque de voyage.

   b. Je peux payer avec une carte de crédit? Non, je regrette, on n'accepte pas les cartes.

   c. Avez-vous ce pull en bleu marine? Non, je regrette, pas en bleu marine.

   d. Vous faites quelle taille? Quarante.

   e. Quelle couleur voulez-vous? Noir.

Unit 6

Pages 88–90

1. Marie-Claude—car, 7:00; Delphine—bike, 7:15; Françoise—school bus, 7:30

2. a. Marie-Claude ne prend pas le bus, elle va en voiture.

   b. Non, elle ne quitte pas la maison à 8h. Elle quitte la maison à 7h30.

3. car, 20 min; bus, a good half hour; train, 45 min; bike, 10 min; subway, 15 min; walking, 2 min.

4. a. (vous) prenez, partez, arrivez; b. (tu) prends, pars, arrives

5. a. aller à pied/c'est bon pour la santé; b. aller en moto/c'est plus pratique; c. aller en voiture/c'est plus confortable; d. prendre le train/c'est plus rapide; e. prendre le bus/c'est moins cher; f. prendre un taxi/il n'y a pas de problème avec le parking; g. prendre le métro/c'est rapide

Pages 92–95

1. a. La Tour Eiffel—le métro, in 5 minutes
b. L'Arc de Triomphe—le bus, in 8 minutes
c. Les Halles—le métro, in 10 minutes
d. La Sacré-Cœur—le métro, every 10 minutes

2. Le musée d'Orsay—line 12, direction Mairie d'Ivry, 10 minutes

La Cité des Sciences—line 7, direction la Courneuve, 20 minutes

Le Louvre—line 8, direction Balard, 20 minutes

Les Halles—line 1, direction Grande Arche de la Défense, 10 minutes

3. l'aéroport, direct; Gare du Nord, changez à la place de la République puis vous prenez le 4; Gare de Lyon, vous prenez le 5 et puis il faut changer à Châtelet, et vous prenez le 6.

5. a. Vous prenez la direction Charles de Gaulle.
b. Vous prenez la direction Châtillon.
c. Vous prenez la direction Porte de la Chapelle.
d. Vous prenez la direction La Courneuve.

Pages 97–100

1&2. 1. theater—taxi; 30 mins, construction
2. Louvre—taxi; 20 mins, traffic
3. Les Etoiles de Nuit—taxi; 10 mins, raining
4. airport—taxi and bus, 60 mins, expensive

3. Je voudrais un taxi pour aller à l'aéroport.
Le vol part à 17h45.
Il met combien de temps?
Ça coûte combien?

4. 1. Quelle sorte de voiture voulez-vous?;
2. Pour combien de personnes?;
3. Comment vous appelez-vous?;
4. Vous voulez la voiture pour combien de jours?;
5. Vous la voulez quand exactement?;
6. Vous avez votre permis de conduire avec vous?;
7. Comment voulez-vous payer?;
8. Votre adresse?

5. 1. Une grande voiture.; 2. Six personnes.;
3. Sylvie Verlaine.; 4. Trois jours.;
5. De vendredi à lundi.; 6. Oui, je l'ai ici.;
7. Avec une carte de crédit.;
8. Hôtel du Parc, rue St-Denis.

Extra 1

1. France—1; Belgique—2; Luxembourg—3; Suisse—4; Mauritanie—5; Sénégal—6; Côte d'Ivoire—7; Guinée—8; Burkina Faso—9; Bénin—10; Niger—11; Tchad—12; République Centrafricaine—13; Cameroun—14; Gabon—15; Congo—16; République Démocratique du Congo—17; Rwanda—18; Burundi—19; Maroc—20; Algérie—21; Tunisie—22; Québec—23; Martinique—24; Guadeloupe—25; St.-Martin—26; Haiti—27

2. M—Suisse, Belgique, Luxembourg, Québec, Martinique, Guadeloupe

O—Mauritainie, Sénégal, Côte d'Ivoire, Guinée, Burkina Faso, Bénin, Niger, Tchad, Republique Centrafricaine, Cameroun, Gabon, Congo, République Démocratique du Congo, Rwanda, Burundi

A—Maroc, Algérie, Tunisie

3. Jean-Marc—Canada; Catherine—Guadeloupe; Noura—Côte d'Ivoire; Benoît—Algérie; Virginie—Suisse; Nadjet—Maroc

Extra 2

1. a. 5; b. 6; c. 1; d. 2; e. 3; f. 4
2. a. €32; b. €99; c. €9,20; d. €5,80; e. €27; f. €27,80; g. €19,50; h. €9,50; i. €49,75

Extra 3

1. 1. On pourrait visiter le parc d'attractions La Ronde.; 2. On pourrait visiter le parc olympique.; 3. On pourrait faire une visite du vieux port ou bien une croisière sur le Saint-Laurent.

2. 1. Visiter le parc d'attractions; 2. Visiter le parc olympique; 3. Visiter le Biôdome; Faire une croisière sur la rivière

3. 1. Aller à la piscine; 2. Aller à la patinoire; 3. Aller au match de foot; 4. Aller au cinéma; 5. Jouer au tennis; 6. Aller en boîte de nuit; 7. Aller au restau

4. 1. Aller au cinéma; 2. Jouer au tennis; 3. Aller en boîte; 4. Aller au restau; 5. Jouer au tennis; 6. Aller au match de hockey

5. 1. avec sa femme; 2. avec son frère; 3. avec sa sœur; 4. avec sa petite amie; 5. avec son petit ami; 6. avec son mari

Extra 4

1. la Soufrière; la plage; Basse Terre; les Cascades

Extra 5

1. 1. Evelyne—sweatshirt, jeans, T-shirt, shorts, swimsuit; 2. Laurent—sweatshirt, jeans, swimsuit, shorts, T-shirt; 3. Maurice—jeans, T-shirt, shorts, sweatshirt, swimsuit, cut-off jeans; 4. Nathalie—jeans, T-shirt, sweatshirt, shorts, bikini

2. a. M. Maillard; b. Mme Crance; c. M. Proudhon; d. M. Dupont; e. Mlle Meugeot; f. Mme Broussard

Extra 6

1. a. Le voyage dure <u>une demi-heure</u>.

b. J'y vais <u>en métro</u>.

c. Je pars <u>à sept heures et quart</u> et je vais <u>à la station de métro</u>.

d. Je prends <u>le métro</u> direction Château de Vincennes, qui passe toutes les <u>cinq</u> minutes.

e. J'arrive à huit heures <u>moins le quart</u>.

3. M. Bernard habite à Genève et va au travail à pied.; Mme Rossi habite à Rome et va au travail en moto.; M. Nicholls habite à New York et va au travail en taxi; Mlle Verlaine va au travail en train; Mme Briand habite à Bruxelles et va au travail en bus.; Mlle Fernandez habite à Madrid et va au travail en voiture.

Test 1

1. 1. b; 2. a; 3. c

2. 1. c; 2. a; 3. d; 4. b

3. f; a; c; d; g; e; b

4. 1. e; 2. d; 3. f; 4. b; 5. a; 6. c

5. 1. l'; 2. le; 3. la; 4. le; 5. l'; 6. la; 7. le; 8. la

6. 1. au; 2. aux; 3. à la; 4. au

7. 1. b; 2. d; 3. g; 4. c; 5. e; 6. a; 7. f

8. je travaille   nous travaillons
tu travailles   vous travaillez
il/elle travaille   ils/elles travaillent

9. 1. la femme; 2. la sœur; 3. la mère; 4. la fille; 5. l'infirmière; 6. la boulangère; 7. l'électricienne; 8. la coiffeuse

10. 1. mon; 2. ma; 3. mon; 4. mes; 5. mon; 6. mon; 7. ma

11. 1. Non, je ne suis pas marié(e).; 2. Il n'habite pas à Paris.; 3. Je ne sais pas!; 4. Je ne travaille pas à mon compte.; 5. Je ne veux pas aller au cinéma.; 6. Elle n'est pas comptable.

Test 2

1. l'arrêt d'autobus—bus stop; l'église (f)—church; la gare—train station; la pharmacie—pharmacy; la station service—gas station; la ville—town

2. 1. d; 2. a; 3. e; 4. b; 5. c

3. 1. à la; 2. à l'; 3. à la; 4. au; 5. au; 6. à l'

4. 1. c; 2. e; 3. a; 4. d; 5. b

5. 1. mon; 2. mes; 3. ma; 4. mon; 5. mes; 6. mon

6. 1. blanche; 2. blanches; 3. blanc; 4. blanche; 5. blancs

7. 1. c; 2. a; 3. b; 4. d

8. 1. il; 2. elle; 3. il; 4. elles; 5. ils; 6. il

9. 1. Vous; 2. Tu; 3. Tu; 4. Vous; 5. Tu; 6. Tu

10. 1. f; 2. d; 3. c; 4. b; 5. e; 6. a.

11. 1. Quelle; 2. combien; 3. Quand; 4. Que; 5. Comment; 6. Où